ACTS

of the

GENERAL CHAPTER OF PROVINCIALS

of the

ORDER OF FRIARS PREACHERS

BOLOGNA

July 16 to August 4, 2016

CELEBRATED UNDER

FR. BRUNO CADORÉ

DOCTOR OF SACRED THEOLOGY

MASTER OF THE ORDER

ROME

CURIA GENERALITIA – SANTA SABINA

2016

Acknowledgements

We gratefully acknowledge the assistance of Fr. James Karepin, O.P., Fr. Thomas Lynch, O.P., and Fr. Vincent Blake, O.P., of the Province of St. Albert the Great, U.S.A., and Br. Herman Johnson, O.P., of the Province of St. Martin de Porres, U.S.A. for their assistance with translations of French and Spanish texts; Fr. Albert Judy, O.P. of the Province of St. Albert the Great, U.S.A., for formatting and editing; and Mrs. Terry Jarbe, Editor of the New Priory Press for production assistance.

Acronyms

ACG	Acta Capituli Generalis
BEST	La Bible en Ses Traditions
CIC	Codex Iuris Canonici
CIDALC	Conferencia Interprovincial Dominicana de América Latina y el Caribe
DSI	Dominican Sisters International
DVI	Dominican Volunteers International
DYM	Dominican Youth Movement (cf. IDYM)
EBAF	École Biblique et Archéologique Française
IAOP	Inter Africa O.P.
IDEO	Institut Dominicain d'Études Orientales – Cairo
IDF	International Dominican Foundation
IDYM	International Dominican Youth Movement - MJDI
IEOP	Inter Europe O.P.
LCO	Liber Constitutionum et Ordinationum Fratrum O.P.
MO	The Master of the Order
OPTIC	Order of Preachers for Technology, Information and Communication
PUST	Pontificia Università San Tommaso d'Aquino Roma
RFG	Ratio Formationis Generalis
RFP	Ratio Formationis Particularis
RSG	Ratio Studiorum Generalis
RSP	Ratio Studiorum Particularis

Editor's Note on the Translation

The *Acts of the 2016 General Chapter of Provincials* were written in Latin and the three official languages of the Order of Preachers: English, French, and Spanish. At New Priory Press, an intellectual ministry of the Province of St. Albert the Great, USA, we are happy once again to produce a full English translation of the Acts. For the sake of the reader, our team of editors and translators have delineated below in which languages the various chapters and sections were originally written, so as to explain any uncommon turns of phrase in the English translation:

English* (original)
> Chapter III: Apostolic Creativity (p. 35); Chapter IV: Restructuring and Collaboration (p. 49); Chapter VII: Constitutions and Ordinations, "LCO" (p. 97) through "Brothers outside community" (p. 98), "Statutes of Vicariates" (p. 98) through "Directories of the Dominican Laity" (p. 99), and "Safeguarding" (p. 100) through "Ordinations of previous general chapters" (p. 103); and Chapter VIII: Economic Commission.

French (original)
> Letter of Promulgation (p. 1); Chapter V: The Life of the Brethren (p. 57); Chapter VII: Constitutions and Ordinations, "Official Languages" (p. 97) and "Permanent Commission for the promotion of studies" (p.99); and Appendix I: *Relatio* on the State of the Order (p.113).

Spanish (original)
> Chapter I: Formalities (p. 11); Chapter II: Prologue (p. 27); Chapter VI: Vocation and Renewal (p. 65); Chapter VII: Constitutions and Ordinations, "Formation in administration" (p. 97) and "Promoters of communications media" (p. 98); Appendix II (p. 167); and Appendix III (p. 171).

Latin (original)
> Membership (p. 7) and Chapter VII: Constitution and Ordinations (p. 73-96).

---

* The English sections within this translation have been reformatted to reflect American English spelling.

Contents

Letter of Promulgation
of Fr. Bruno Cadoré OP
Humble Master and Servant
of the Entire Order of Preachers

My very dear Brothers in Saint Dominic,

By this letter, I promulgate the Acts of the General Chapter celebrated at Bologna (Italy) from July 16th through August 4th, 2016. As the Prologue tells us, this Chapter invites us to make this year, when we celebrate the Jubilee of the Order and of the extraordinary Year of Mercy, the first step toward renewing our vocation as preachers. By sending us forth to follow in the footsteps of the first seventy-two disciples sent out by Jesus, to preach grace and mercy, [Lk 10:1-20] the Chapter invites us to be watchful guardians, with one another and for one another, of that vocation which links us, transforming our diversity into unity.

At the close of the Chapter, I recalled before the assembly the scene recounted in the first Book of Kings where the prophet Elijah, while waiting on the mountainside "for God to come by," finally recognized Him "in the soft whisper of a gentle breeze," [1 Kgs 19:12]. Zeal for the Lord emboldened the prophet and, so great was his passion for the covenant promised by God, that he was able to confront earthquake and fire and hurricane there on the mountainside where he kept vigil. Such events are not foreign to the world into which we are sent out to preach today, and they seem capable of undermining the security of persons and peoples, of dashing all hope of building human communities based on peace and mercy, of using division and confrontation to thwart any who would seek wisdom and a spiritual life. But the boldness of the prophet does not consist primarily in opposing these realities; his task is rather to learn how to recognize, amid suffering, "the soft whisper" of the Word, of the promise, and of the coming of the grace which patiently shapes the world "for God." In a sense, God's humility receives in response that of the prophet who finds therein the strength and boldness which are his zeal and his passion for God's covenant.

1

In many places and in many ways, the brothers and the sisters of the Order are like Elijah keeping vigil on the mountainside. Along with those tied to them by apostolic fellowship, they experience absurd and divisive violence, halting discussions among cultures and religions, social inequalities, fraying relations among nations, breakdowns of trust with regard to their fellows or to institutions, fundamental changes in the ways people communicate, and difficulties finding a common basis for visioning together a world which belongs to all. Sharing these cares for the world with so many others, not only in their ministerial commitments but also within their familial and cultural bastions, they often get the feeling that evangelization is not easily accomplished within these contexts. We must be patient, taking our time and using all available means to listen more and more; we must be driven to seek better to understand the implications of these complex realities; we must be humble enough to accept that, in many cases, the human words which offer promise are but stutters. Apostolic boldness is thus not to shirk away from the call to recognize the task of mercy and the grace of salvation in this world, but rather to take the risk of offering ourselves as servants charged with this task.

It is in this sense, I believe, that the Acts of this Chapter invite us to the exacting task of *renewing our personal and communal vocation.* The stakes outlined above emphasize how necessary it is carefully to cultivate the vineyard entrusted to us, promoting new vocations for the Order and for all branches of the Dominican Family. But this effort will find both strength and meaning to the extent that each and all commit to a renewal of the vocation of preacher at this moment in the history of the world and of the Church. With an eye to this, the Chapter reaffirms the role of the community project, of community visitations, and of the attention which we must always pay to dialogue among us and to steps aimed at reconciliation among us.

The Chapter concretely manifested the importance of this dimension by establishing the post of Socius to the Master of the Order for Fraternal Life and Formation. Within the General Council, this socius will be responsible for helping to promote the renewal of initial and permanent formation according to the new *Ratio Formationis Generalis.* He will also contribute to a task imposed by the Chapter, namely, integrating the reality of aging into our thinking, seeing it as a specific stage in the living out of our vocation. He will also participate in the continuing reflection concerning the specific vocation of cooperator

2

brothers within the Order, whose role is clearly being recognized as indispensable.

Following the insights already affirmed by the Chapters of Rome and Trogir, the Chapter of Bologna reaffirmed that the renewal of our vocation called us to renew our understanding of the link between brotherhood and mission. It is in this sense that there has been a reaffirmation of a restructuring of the entities making up the Order – provinces (or vice provinces) and provincial vicariates: these latter, it has been maintained, shall be accorded a certain participation at General Chapters; the Chapter also insisted that they be integrated into the life of the province, and that they play a role in the mission of the worldwide Order. Since this restructuring aims at reinforcing the synergy between fraternal life and mission, it deals with much more than merely a definition of the entities. Several points were brought out by the Chapter.

The first of these concerns *the worldwide nature of the Order's vocation* – underlined insistently by the young student brothers, who met with the capitulars just after they had finished their pilgrimage, *In the Footsteps of Saint Dominic*. Each entity should take to heart the expanding horizon calling us to apostolic and missionary concern, thereby reinforcing the image of an Order which promotes an ever greater synergy among the provinces with an eye toward our common preaching mission. It is this horizon which will best enliven *the spirit of collaboration*, expressed in many ways and aimed at several dimensions of the Order (apostolic collaboration, youth and vocational ministry, initial and permanent formation, study, and the ministry of teaching and research). It is now up to the entities, and to the availability of the brothers, to concretely manifest this desire for collaboration, for intercultural exchange, and for an increased international identity, which the capitulars have affirmed.

Restructuring in the realms of study and research has been strongly emphasized, in particular concerning the institutions under the direct jurisdiction of the Master of the Order, including their links to the various study centers, which exist within the provinces. In this area, two projects received encouragement – one in Asia and the other in Africa. Moreover, setting in motion such a collaboration calls for a certain creativity which can promote a genuine *culture of solidarity*. The Chapter insisted on the necessity of providing the concrete means required for such solidarity – not only economically, but also in terms of assignments, of mobility, of joint apostolic projects, and of exchanges planned for the years of initial formation.

Finally, the brothers of the chapter emphasized the fact that this renewal of the "apostolic structures" should not only apply to the overall organization of the Order, but also *to each of the entities, seeking continually to adapt its structures better to new needs wherever its mission might call.* How can we better provide the means not only to maintain our current realities, but also to risk bold new initiatives without fearing the uncertainty, which sometimes arise as we seek a response that is better adapted to a changing context?

The entire thrust of this renewal is aimed at the preaching mission which, in the present context and in every corner of the globe, demands a genuinely apostolic creativity. This creativity should spring from, as well as being inspired and strengthened by, a demanding spirituality of listening and of encountering, which must characterize the relationships among the brothers as much as it does the way in which they enter into conversation with the world. This spirituality must be at the heart of a process by which local and provincial projects are worked out. The Chapter set forth five areas where apostolic creativity is especially to be expected: the dialogue with religions and cultures, ecology, the dialogue between faith and science, the digital world, and the fact of indifference. With regard to this latter, the Acts ask us to undertake research on a scale which engages the entire Order.

The Acts stress certain aspects of the apostolic life upon which we should focus particular attention: the impetus toward establishing new foundations and the choices which this might entail; the possibility of new apostolic collaborations involving various members of the Dominican family (as, for instance, in setting up "Dominican ministry centers,") along with the mutual support which the different branches of the Dominican family can offer one another; caring together for missions which are new, or which, for all their importance to our common preaching ministry, are located within challenging contexts; the specific contribution of cooperator brothers to our common mission; and the importance of international projects.

The Chapter also wanted to encourage all brothers to take part in renewing currently functioning missions, emphasizing the importance of ministerial linkages being set up in the wake of the Chapter of Trogir; these should allow the brothers to engage in sharing and to reflect together upon their ministerial commitments. This impetus will be further intensified at the Congress for the Order's Mission, which will conclude the Jubilee Year, and which will promote a dialogue between apostolic life and theological reflection – precisely the nucleus of our vocation as preachers.

From brotherhood to mission, and from mission to brotherhood. This is indeed the path opened up by the sending out of the disciples presented in the Gospel of Luke and commented upon in the Prologue. In the course of our meeting with Pope Francis, the Holy Father insisted on the link between witness and preaching. Commenting upon the fact that Dominic sold his books to care for the poor, he strongly invited us to keep our ears open to Christ's living flesh which thirsts for a genuine and liberating Word and, listening to the cry "I thirst," constitutes the main axis of our mission, and is the basic criterion for adjusting our "structures." It is also the key to renewing our vocation as preachers of grace and mercy.

On the [Feast of the] Solemnity of Saint Dominic
Rome, August 8, 2016

fr. Bruno Cadoré, o.p.
Maître de l'Ordre

fr. Franklin Buitrago Rojas, o.p.
a secretis

Prot. 50/16/ 558 Bologna 2016

Membership
Under Fr. Bruno Cadoré, op
Master of the Entire Order of Preachers

Priors Provincial

fr. Jesús Antonio DÍAZ SARIEGO, *Province of Hispania*

fr. Loïc Marie LE BOT, *Province of Tolouse*

fr. Michel LACHENAUD, *Province of France*

fr. Fausto ARICI, *Province of St. Dominic in Italy*

fr. Aldo TARQUINI, *Province of St. Catharine of Siena, Rome*

fr. Francesco LA VECCHIA, *Province of St. Thomas Aquinas in Italy*

fr. Johannes BUNNENBERG, *Province of Germany*

fr. Martin GANERI, *Province of England*

fr. Paweł KOZACKI, *Province of Poland*

fr. Benedikt Tomáš MOHELNÍK, *Province of Bohemia*

fr. Anto GAVRIĆ, *Province of the Annunciation of the BVM in Croatia*

fr. Pedro DA CRUZ FERNANDES, *Province of Portugal*

fr. René L. DINKLO, *Province of Netherlands*

fr. Gregory CARROLL, *Province of Ireland*

fr. Jorge Rafael DIAZ NUÑEZ, *Province of St. James in México*

fr. Juan José SALAVERRY VILLARREAL, *Province of St. John the Baptist in Peru*

fr. Said LEÓN AMAYA, *Province of San Luis Beltrán in Colombia*

fr. Javier GONZÁLEZ IZQUIERDO, *Province of Our Lady of the Rosary*

fr. Javier María POSE, *Province of St. Augustine, Argentina*

fr. Kenneth Raymond LETOILE, *Province of St. Joseph in the U.S.A.*

fr. Frans MICALLEF, *Province of St. Pius V, Malta*

fr. André DESCÔTEAUX, *Province of St. Dominic, Canada*

fr. Mark C. PADREZ, *Province of The Most Holy Name in the U.S.A.*

fr. Thomas G. BROGL, *Province of Upper Germany and Austria*

fr. James Vincent MARCHIONDA, *Province of St. Albert the Great in the U.S.A.*

fr. Kevin SAUNDERS, *Province of the Assumption of the BVM, Australia and New Zealand*

fr. Edivaldo António DOS SANTOS, *Province of fr. Bartholomé de Las Casas in Brazil*

fr. Guido VERGAUWEN, *Province of the Annunciation of the BVM in Switzerland*

fr. Joseph NGUYEN DUC HOA, *Province of The Queen of Martyrs in Vietnam*

fr. Gerard Francisco P. TIMONER III, *Province of Philippines*

fr. Thomas M. CONDON, *Province of St. Martin de Porres in the U.S.A.*
fr. Carlos Antonio CACERES PEREIRA, *Province of St. Vincent Ferrer in Central America*
fr. Charles UKWE, *Province of St. Joseph the Worker in Nigeria*
fr. John KUSUMALAYAM, *Province of India*
fr. Reginald Adrián SLAVKOVSKÝ, *Province of Slovakia*

Vice Provincials

fr. Armando Alonso VILLALTA SALAZAR, *Vice Province of St. Catharine of Siena, Ecuador*
fr. Philippe COCHINAUX, *Vice Province of St. Thomas Aquinas in Belgium*
fr. Pascal Paulus NAZIR MASIH, *Vice Province of the Sons of Mary in Pakistan*
fr. Bienvenu NSEKOKO BONGO, *Vice Province of the Democratic Republic of the Congo*
fr. Benjamin Sombel SARR, *Vice Province of St. Augustine in West Africa*
fr. Fernando DELGADO FLÓREZ, *Vice Province of Bolivia*

Vicars General

fr. Miguel Angel RÍOS VIVANCO, *Vicar General of St. Laurence the Martyr in Chile*
fr. Stanislaus MUYEBE, *Vicar General of South Africa*
fr. Vincent LI, *Vicar General of the Queen of China*

Delegates of the Vicariates

fr. Jean Paul KAMAHEU, *Vicariate of Equatorial Africa – Province of France*
fr. Mariano GONZALEZ MARTIN, *Vicariate of Japan – Province of Our Lady of the Rosary*
fr. Jean MIYAMOTO, *Vicariate of Japan – Province of St. Dominic, Canada*
fr. Marcel BRAEKERS, *Vicariate of St. Rose in Flanders – Vice Province of St. Thomas Aquinas in Belgium*
fr. Peter PHAM, *Vicariate of Canada – Province of The Queen of Martyrs, Vietnam*

Delegate of the Convents under the Immediate Jurisdiction of the Master of the Order

fr. Bernhard BLANKENHORN, *Convent of Saints Dominic and Sixtus, Rome*

Other Participants at the General Chapter

Assistants of the Master of the Order and the Syndic of the Order
fr. Orlando RUEDA ACEVEDO, *Socius for the Apostolic Life*
fr. Michael MASCARI, *Socius for the Intellectual Life*
fr. Vincent LU HA, *Socius for the provinces of Asia and the Pacific*
fr. Krzysztof POPLAWSKI, *Socius for the provinces in Central and Eastern Europe*
fr. Miguel Angel DEL RIO GONZALEZ, *Socius for the provinces in the Iberian Peninsula and the Italian provinces and Malta*
fr. Hilario PROVECHO ALVAREZ, *Syndic of the Order*
fr. Eric SALOBIR, *Promoter for Media*

Brothers invited by the Master of the Order
fr. Roberto CLARK, *Cooperator Brother*
fr. Mariusz SKOWRONSKI, *Cooperator Brother*
fr. Jean Jacques PERENNES, *Director the École Biblique, Jerusalem*
fr. Benjamin EARL, *Canon Law Expert*

Invited by the Master of the Order from the Dominican Family
sr. M. Vincenza PANZA, *Nun*
sr. Marie Juliette KILANIR, *Nun*
sr. Marie Thérèse CLEMENT, *International Coordinator of the DSI*
sr. Marie-Jean MOUTON-BRADY, *The Roman Congregation of St. Dominic*
Mr. Hector MARQUEZ, *Dominican Laity*
Rev. Jesper FICH, *Priestly Brotherhood*
Mr. Jose Alberto DE BLAS MONCALVILLO, *IDYM*

Moderators
fr. Leobardo ALMAZAN
fr. Alain ARNOULD
fr. John O'CONNOR

Secretary
fr. Roberto GIORGIS, *General Secretary*

Interpreters
fr. Alejandro CROSTHWAITE
fr. Juan TORRES
fr. Cristóbal TORRES
fr. Olivier POQUILLON
fr. Thomas-Marie GILLET
fr. Carlos Ma. IZAGUIRRE
fr. José Rafael REYES GONZALEZ
sr. Laetitia YOUTCHENKO
fr. Paul Dominique MASSICLAT
fr. Matthew JARVIS
fr. Carlos QUIJANO
fr. Jean Ariel BAUZA SALINAS
fr. Jesús MOLONGWA
fr. Neil FERGUSON
sr. Marie-Imelda BAUDIN DE LA VALETTE
fr. Sixto CASTRO
fr. Didier CROONENBERGHS
fr. Emilio GARCIA ÁLVAREZ
fr. Bruno CLIFTON

Assistants
fr. MAXIMILIANO CAPPABIANCA, Cantor of the General Chapter
fr. Daniele DRAGO
fr. Davide PEDONE
fr. Matteo MONTALCINI
fr. Mario ABETE
fr. Alessandro AMPRINO
fr. Daniele CASSANI
fr. Adriano CAVALLO
fr. Andrea CODIGNOLA
fr. Emanuele FACCIOLO

fr. Gregorio KIM
fr. Francesco LOMBARDO
fr. Gianluca LOPEZ
fr. Luca REFATTI
fr. Filippo RUBINI
fr. Massimo VERONESE
Mr. Florent de SUREMAIN
Ms. Maria CAMPONE

Chapter I: Formalities

1. We report that, with a circular letter dated in Rome on November 15, 2015, the Master of the Order, fr. Bruno Cadoré, under LCO 413 §II, convoked the General Chapter of Priors Provincial held in the city of Bologna (Italy), from July 16 to August 4, 2016.

2. We report that the Master of the Order, under LCO 414, appointed fr. Roberto Giorgis as Secretary General of the Chapter on July 14, 2014.

3. We report that the Master of the Order, fr. Bruno Cadoré, invited to the General Chapter of Priors Provincial in Bologna, fr. Roberto Clark and fr. Mariusz Skowronski, cooperator brothers; fr. Jean Jacques Perennes, Director of the EBAF; and fr. Benjamin Earl, an expert in Canon Law.

4. We report that the following members of the Dominican Family attended the General Chapter as guests of the Master of the Order: Sr. M. Vincenza Panza, nun of the Monastery of Azzano-S Paolo (Italy); Sr. Marie Juliette Kilanir, nun of the Monastery of Bambui (Cameroon); Sr. Marie Thérèse Clement, President of Dominican Sisters International; Sister Marie-Jean Mouton-Brady of the Roman Congregation of St. Dominic; Mr. Hector Marquez, President of the International Council of Lay Dominican Fraternities; P. Jesper Fich of the Priestly Fraternities of St. Dominic; and Mr. José Alberto de Blas Moncalvillo from the Dominican International Youth Movement.

5. We report that on June 15, 2016, the Master of the Order, fr. Bruno Cadoré, sent a letter to Pope Francis, acknowledging the celebration of the General Chapter in Bologna.

Rome, 15 June 2016
His Holiness Pope Francis Vatican City

Prot 50/16/417 Bologna_2016

Most Holy Father,

As already indicated to His Holiness, the Order of Preachers is preparing to celebrate its General Chapter (a Chapter of Provincials) from July 15 to August 4, 2016 and I would humbly ask you to grant your apostolic blessing for the brothers who will gather in Bologna.

This Chapter is celebrated precisely at the midpoint of our celebration of the 8th centenary of the confirmation of the Order by Pope Honorius III, a celebration that was opened on November 7 last year and will close with a Eucharistic celebration at St. John Lateran on January 21, 2017.

We see it as a special grace, and a challenging call, that in God's Providence our celebration coincides with the Year of Mercy celebrated in the Church universal. That Mercy has always been at the heart of Dominican preaching, following the example and sharing the concerns of St. Dominic, the preacher of grace, showing always compassion for the poor, defending the truth of creation and human dignity, and preaching tirelessly for the salvation of mankind.

This period of preparation, and the time of the chapter itself, are for the brothers, sisters, and lay people of the Order, a favorable period for responding eagerly to his call to all the faithful to live mercy always and in every situation. The Order wants to make its contribution to the construction of the "revolution of tenderness" of which you have spoken.

During our Chapter, the World Youth Days will be hosted in Poland and we I assure you that we will be in communion with you at such an important moment in the life of the Church.

And at the end of the Chapter it will be our great pleasure to come to Rome to be received in audience by His Holiness, a thing for which I would like again to express my sincere gratitude.

Thanking you in advance for your blessing, I wish to express my gratitude for your ministry and assure you of my prayers and my respectful and fraternal greetings.

fr. Bruno Cadoré, op
Master of the Order of Preachers

6. We report that on July 15, the Secretary of State of His Holiness Pope Francis sent the following telegram to the Master of the Order and the Chapter:

CHAPTER I: FORMALITIES

Fr. Bruno Cadoré OP
Master General of the Order of Preachers
Convent of Santa Sabina

On the occasion of the General Chapter of Provincials of the Order of Preachers, which is held in Bologna, in the context of the extraordinary Jubilee of Mercy of the eighth centenary of the confirmation of the Order by Pope Honorius III, Pope Francis, returning his cordial good wishes, invokes the divine gifts of the Spirit, remembering that the keystone which sustains the life of the Church is mercy. Everything in its pastoral action must be wrapped in tenderness and nothing of his announcement and his testimony to the world can be lacking in mercy. The credibility of the Church passes through the path of merciful and compassionate love which gives new life and infuses courage to view the future with hope.

The Holy Father hopes that those who follow the charism of Saint Dominic, a tireless apostle of grace and forgiveness, compassion toward the poor and staunch defender of truth, should give testimony to this mercy, professing and embodying it in life and as a sign of closeness and the tenderness of God, so that even today's society may rediscover the urgency of solidarity, love and forgiveness.

He, while asking for prayers in support of his Petrine ministry, through the intercession of Our Lady of the Rosary and of all the saints of the Dominican family, imparts to you and to the capitular confreres the requested Apostolic Blessing, which I willingly extend to the entire Order.

From the Vatican July 15, 2016.
Cardinal Pietro Parolin
Secretary of State of His Holiness

7. We report that fr. Loïc-Marie Le Bot, fr. Gregory Carroll and fr. Said Leon Amay, on the afternoon of July15th and the morning of July 16th, have examined the testimonial letters of the vocals.

8. We report that fr. Timothy Radcliffe, former Master of the Order, has asked to be excused from participation in the General Chapter for health reasons.

9. We report that in the afternoon of July 15, a group of 114 student brothers and sisters in formation, at the end of their pilgrimage, "In the Footsteps of St. Dominic," joined the procession of capitulars from the Rotunda of Madonna del Monte, site of the former Benedictine convent, to our convent of Saint Dominic. After the procession, Compline was sung and a procession was made to the altars of the Blessed Virgin Mary and St. Dominic.

10. We report that the General Chapter began on July 16, 2016 with the High Mass of the Holy Spirit, concelebrated by the Chapter and presided over by the Master of the Order, fr. Bruno Cadoré. Student friars and sisters on the pilgrimage, "In the Footsteps of St. Dominic," also participated in the solemn opening Mass of the Chapter.

In his homily, the Master of the Order invited the Chapter members to spend the time of the Chapter following the invitation of Jesus to his disciples: "Come away by yourselves to a deserted place and rest a while," (Mk 6:31). He explained that a General Chapter is a time to let the Holy Spirit work in us, listening to each other, learning compassion from Jesus, listening to the hopes of the people to whom we are sent to preach, asking the Holy Spirit to make our communities "parables of communion."

11. We report that on the afternoon of July 16, the Chapter met with the student brothers and sisters on the pilgrimage, "In the Footsteps of St. Dominic." They presented to the General Chapter some reflections, proposals and concerns raised along the pilgrimage and then deepened the dialogue in their different linguistic groups.

12. We report that on July 16, the Master of the Order, having heard the opinion of the chapter as provided by LCO 417 § I,3, appointed as reviewers of the text of the Acts of the General Chapter, fr. Martin Ganeri, provincial of England; fr. Benjamin Sombel Sarr, vice provincial of West Africa; and fr. Javier Gonzalez Izquierdo, provincial of the Province of the Most Holy Rosary.

13. We report that the Master of the Order, having consulted the Chapter according to LCO 417 § I,4, confirmed the previously prepared distribution of members and the chairmen of the eight commissions:

COMMISSION 1: APOSTOLIC CREATIVITY *(English)*
fr. James MARCHIONDA (35) *(Chairman)*
fr. Pawel KOZACKI (10)
fr. Kenneth R. LETOILE (29)
fr. Frans MICALLEF (30)
fr, Guido VERGAUWEN (38) *(Secretary)*
fr. Benjamin Sombel SARR (84)
fr. Peter Huong PHAM (40)
fr. Mariusz SKOWRONSKI *(10, invited)*
sr. Marie Juliette KILANIR *(guest)*
Jesper P. FICH *(guest)*
fr. Vincent LU HA *(40, Socius of the Master for the provinces of Asia
    and Pacific)*

COMMISSION 2: RESTRUCTURING AND COLLABORATION *(English)*
fr. Philippe COCHINAUX (39) *(Chairman)*
fr. Michel LACHENAUD (03)
fr. Johannes BUNNENBERG (08)
fr. Martin GANERI (09) *(Secretary)*
fr. Gregory CARROLL (18)
fr. Kevin SAUNDERS (36)
fr. Joseph Duc Hoa NGUYEN (40)
fr. Vincent LI (49)
fr. Bernhard BLANKENHORN *(32, convents delegated under the
    immediate jurisdiction of the Master)*
sr. Therese Marie CLEMENT (guest)
fr. Michael MASCARI *(35, Socius of the Master for Intellectual Life)*
fr. Krzysztof POPŁAWSKI *(10, Socius of the MO for the provinces in
    Central and Eastern Europe)*

COMMISSION 3: LIFE OF THE FRIARS; COMMON LIFE AND
    GOVERNMENT *(in French)*
fr. Fausto ARICI (04) *(Chairman)*
fr. Jean-Paul KAMAHEU (03) *(Secretary)*
fr. Francesco LAVECCHIA (06)
fr. Benedikt Thomàs MOHELNÍK (12)
fr. Anto GAVRIC (13)
fr. Jean MIYAMOTO (31)
fr. Marcel BRAEKERS (39)
fr. Carlos CÁCERES (44)
fr. Reginald Adrian SLAVKOVSKY (83)

fr. Pascal Paulus NAZIR (43)
fr. Bienvenu NSEKOKO BONGO (84)
sr. Marie-Jean MOUTON-BRADY *(guest)*

COMMISSION 4: APOSTOLIC CREATIVITY *(in Spanish)*
fr. Fernando DELGADO FLOREZ (85) *(Chairman)*
fr. Jesus Antonio DIAZ SARIEGO (01)
fr. Pedro DA CRUZ FERNANDES (15)
fr. Jorge Rafael DÍAZ NÚÑEZ (19) *(Secretary)*
fr. Said LEÓN AMAYA (21)
fr. Mark PADREZ (32)
fr. Jean-Jacques PERENNES *(03, Guest)*
fr. Roberto CLARK *(28 Guest)*
Mr. Hector MÁRQUEZ *(guest)*
Mr. José Alberto DE BLAS MONCALVILLO *(guest)*
fr. Orlando RUEDA ACEVEDO *(21, Socius of the Master for Apostolic Life)*

COMMISSION 5: VOCATIONS AND RENEWAL *(in Spanish)*
fr. Armando VILLALTA SALAZAR (23) *(Chairman)*
fr. Aldo TARQUINI (05)
fr. Thomas BROGL (34)
fr. Thomas CONDON (42)
fr. Edivaldo Antonio DOS SANTOS (37)
fr. John KUSUMALAYAM (46)
fr. Gerard Francisco TIMONER (41)
fr. Miguel Angel RIOS VIVANCO (24)
fr. Mariano GONZÁLEZ MARTÍN (25) *(Secretary)*
sr. Maria Vincenza PANZA *(guest)*
fr. Miguel Angel DEL RÍO GONZALEZ *(01, Socius of the MO for the provinces of the Iberian Peninsula, Italy and Malta)*

COMMISSION 6: LCO *(English)*
fr. Loïc-Marie LE BOT (02) *(Chairman)*
fr. Javier GONZALEZ IZQUIERDO (25)
fr. Javier POSE (28) *(Secretary)*
fr. Charles UKWE (45)
fr. Benjamin EARL *(09, Expert in Canon Law)*

COMMISSION 7: ECONOMICS *(English and Spanish)*
fr. André DESCÔTEAUX (31) *(Chairman)*

fr. René DINKLO (17) *(Secretary)*
fr. Juan José SALAVERRY VILLAREAL (20)
fr. Stanislas MUYEBE (48)
fr. Hilario PROVECHO ÁLVAREZ *(01, Syndic of the Order)*

14. We report that on July 16, the General Chapter approved the moderators for plenary sessions: fr. John O'Connor of the Province of England, fr. Leobardo Almazan of the Province of St. Martin de Porres, USA, and fr. Alain Arnould of the Vice Province of St. Thomas, Belgium, previously proposed by the Master of the Order.

15. We report that the Chapter approved the general procedural rules proposed in due course to the Chapter friars.

16. We report that the Master of the Order, fr. Bruno Cadoré, presented his *Report on the State of the Order* to the Capitulars, signed in Rome on December 22, 2015 (cf. Appendix I).

17. We report that the Socius of the Master of the Order as well as the General Syndic and other officials of the Order presented their reports, which were made available to the members of the Chapter.

18. We report that the Master of the Order, fr. Bruno Cadoré, after the General Chapter of Trogir in 2013, made the following appointments:

Socii:
fr. Miguel Ángel del Rio González, Socius for the provinces of the Iberian Peninsula and Socius for the provinces of Italy and Malta (10/07/14).
fr. Javier Maria Pose: Socius for the provinces of Latin America and the Caribbean (02/07/14).
fr. Luis Javier Rubio Guerrero: Socius for the provinces of Latin America and the Caribbean (04/01/16), after the election of Fr. Javier Pose as provincial of Argentina.
fr. Kzrysztof Popławski: Socius for the provinces of Central and Eastern Europe (10/08/14).
fr. Orlando Rueda Acevedo: Socius for Apostolic Life (11/19/14).

General Promoters:
fr. Rui Carlos Antunes e Almeida Lopes was appointed General
    Promoter for the Laity (09/04/13).
fr. César Valero, General Promoter of the Nuns (01/15/14).
fr. Michael Christopher Deeb: Promoter of Justice and Peace
    (10/25/14).

Other officials:
fr. Florentino Bolo: Coordinator for Priestly Fraternities of the Order
    (10/12/13).
fr. Gaspar de Roja Sigaya: Archivist of the Order (10/16/13).
fr. Franklin Buitrago Rojas: Coordinator of the Jubilee of the Order
    (11/23/13).
fr. Michael Christopher Deeb: Delegate to the United Nations
    (01/09/14).
fr. Viliam Doci: Director of the Historical Institute of the Order
    (06/25/15).
fr. Gianni Festa: Postulator General of the Order (11/17/15).
fr. Llewellyn Muscat: Secretary of the Postulator General of the Order
    (12/14/15).

fr. Jose Filipe Da Costa, fr. David Caron, fr. Thomas Moller, fr. Dominik
Jurczak, sr. Ragnhild Bjelland: ordinary members of the Liturgical
Commission of the Order (07/14/14) and fr. Joseph Nguyen Van Hien
and fr. Manuel Eduardo Solorzano as adjunct members (07/14/14).

fr. Augustin Laffay, fr. Luciano Cinelli and fr. Viliam Doci: members of
the Commission for the renewal of the Historical Institute of the Order
(09/14/13).

fr. Ignatius Perkins, fr. Robert Clark, fr. José Bolabato Bolebanza, fr.
Jacques Ambec, fr. Joseph Mai Van Tuyen and fr. Maciej Nitecki:
coordinating committee to promote the renewal and advancement of
the study on the cooperator brothers developed in 2013 (12/02/13). fr.
Roberto Clark was appointed chairman of that committee.

fr. Carlos Ariel Betancourth, fr. Anto Boks, fr. Richar Ounsworth, fr.
Kenneth Siccard, fr. Paolo Venturelli, fr. Richard Ogedengbe (02/13/14)
and fr. Adam Sulikowski (03/20/12) as members of the Economic
Council of the Order.

fr. Dominic Izzo, fr. Roger Houngbedji, fr. Philippe Cochinaux, fr. Juan Luis Mediavilla (03/09/14) and fr. Rolando de la Rosa (01/13/16) as members of the Board of *Spem Miram International*.

Mr. Duncan MacLaren as a member of the International Commission of Justice and Peace (07/21/16).

Sr. Marie-Therese Clement, fr. Martin Ganeri, fr. Darren Dias, fr. Jean Druel, fr. Robini Marianti, fr. Orlando Rueda, fr. Michael Mascari as members of the Commission for Interreligious Dialogue (09/29/14).

19. We report that on January 7, 2014, the Master of the Order issued Decree of Suppression of the General Vicariate of the Guardian Angels in the Baltics and assigned the responsibility for the mission of the Order in this territory to the Province of France.

20. We report that on March 11, 2014, the Master of the Order stated that the General Vicariate of St. Thomas Aquinas in Belgium met the requirements to be a vice province and enjoyed privileges and corresponding obligations.

21. We report that on August 8, 2014, the Master of the Order stated that the General Vicariate of Santa Catalina de Siena of Ecuador met the requirements to be a vice province and enjoyed privileges and corresponding obligations.

22. We report that on August 8, 2015, the Master of the Order issued the decree that beginning 1 January 2016 the provinces of Spain, Aragon and Bética be joined in one province called Hispania.

23. We report that the September 14, 2015, the Master of the Order issued the decree that as of September 28, 2015 the House, St. Catherine of Alexandria, St. Petersburg, was separated from the General Vicariate of Russia and Ukraine to be placed under the jurisdiction of the Province of Poland.

24. We report that on September 25, 2015, the Master of the Order issued the decree that the Santa Rosa Flanders province was abolished and gave responsibility for the mission of the Order in that territory to the Vice Province of St. Thomas Aquinas, Belgium. The decree came into effect on September 27, 2015.

25. We report that on November 23, 2015, the Master of the Order issued the decree which began on January 1, 2016 to suppress the General Vicariate of Santa Cruz of Puerto Rico and the mission of the Order in that territory be given to the Province of San Luis Beltrán of Colombia.

26. We report that on November 23, 2015, the Master of the Order issued the decree on June 7, 2016 that the General Vicariate of Russia and Ukraine was suppressed and he assigned the responsibility for the mission of the Order in that territory to the Province of Poland.

27. We report that on November 27, 2015, the Master of the Order issued the decree beginning January 18, 2016, to suppress the General Vicariate of Hungary and gave the responsibility for the mission of the Order in that territory to the Province of Teutonia.

28. We report that on May 31, 2016, the Master of the Order stated that the General Vicariate of San Pius V of the Democratic Republic of Congo met the requirements to be a vice province and enjoyed the privileges and corresponding obligations.

29. We report that on December 22, 2013, the Master of the Order addressed a letter to the entire Dominican family: *"The Dominican Laity and Preaching."*

30. We report that on May 24, 2014, the Master of the Order addressed the entire Dominican family in a letter: *"Mendicants and being in solidarity with others: For a culture of solidarity at the service of preaching."*

31. We report that on February 2, 2015, the Master of the Order addressed the entire Dominican family in a letter: *"Dominic: Government, Spirituality and Freedom."*

32. We report that on September 21, 2015, the Master of the Order addressed the friars of the Order in a letter: *"From the 'Propositum' of the Order to the conventual project of apostolic life." (cf.* ACG Trogir 2013 69).

33. We report that on September 21, 2015, for the solemn opening of the Jubilee, the Master of the Dominican Order addressed the letter *"Sent to Preach the Gospel,"* to the whole Dominican Family.

34. We report that on January 1, 2016, the Master of the Order addressed the entire Dominican family in the letter: *"'Woe to me if I do not preach the gospel,' (1 Cor 9:16) The Order of Preachers, Yesterday, Today, and Tomorrow."*

35. We report that during the past three years, the Master of the Order made canonical visits to the Province of St. Joseph, USA (09/10/13–09/18/13), to the Province of India (10/15/13 to 10/31/13), to the Vice Province of St. Augustine of Africa (11/05/13–11/14/13), to the community of San Clemente in Rome of the Province of Ireland (12/02/13), to the Province of Ireland (12/03/13–12/15/13), to the Province of England (12/15/13–12/23/13), to the Province of St. Thomas in Italy (01/07/14–01/20/14), to the Province of Malta and its community in Albania (01/24/14–02/01/14), to the Province of Switzerland (02/03/14–02/07/14), to the Province of St. Dominic in Italy (02/08/14–02/21/14), to the Roman Province of St. Catherine of Siena (03/14/14–03/27/14), to the community of the Most Holy Trinity in Rome of the Province of the Most Holy Rosary (03/31/14), to the Province of Aragon (04/02/14–04/14/14), to the Convent of St. Stephen in Jerusalem (04/16/13–04/20/13), to the Province of Bética (04/27/14–05/06/14), to the Vicariate of the Province of The Most Holy Rosary in Spain (05/05/14–05/07/14), to the Province of Spain (06/08/14–06/30/14), to the Vice Province of Bolivia (08/18/14–08/27/14), to the Province of Teutonia (09/14/14–09/29/14), to the Province of Vietnam (10/03/14–10/22/14), to the Province of St. Albert the Great, USA (10/26/14–11/10/14), to the Convent of Saints Dominic and Sixtus in Rome (11/29/14–12/03/14), to the Province of Nigeria (12/04/14–12/22/14), to the Leonine Commission (01/12/15–01/15/15), to the General Vicariate of Russia and Ukraine (02/01/15–02/05/15), to the Convent of St. Albert the Great in Freiburg (02/10/15–02/13/15), to Belarus (03/07/15–03/10/15), to the Pontifical University of St. Thomas in Rome (03/23/15–03/24/15), to Bartolomé de las Casas Province of Brazil (04/14/15–04/29/15), to the General Vicariate of Chile (04/30/15–05/04/15), to the Province of St. John the Baptist, Peru, and the Vicariate of Santa Rosa, Province of Spain (06/02/15–

06/19/15), to the Convent of the Province of France in Cairo (06/29/15–07/01/15), to the Province of Mexico (07/28/15–08/11/15), to the Vicariate of the Province of St. Dominic in Turkey (09/22/15–09/24/15), to the Vice Province of Pakistan (11/30/15–12/09/15), to the house of the Province of Spain in Equatorial Guinea (12/16/15–12/18/15), to the Convent of the Province of Toulouse on the island of Réunion (12/19/15–12/23/15), to the Province of Toulouse (01/15/16–01/18/16), to the Province of Colombia (01/22/16–02/03/16), to the Province of Bohemia (02/28/16–03/02/16), to the Province of Slovakia (03/13/16–03/19/16), to the Vice Province of Ecuador (05/02/16–05/08/16), to the General Vicariate of Our Lady, Queen of China (05/31/16–06/11/16) and to the General Vicariate of South Africa (06/19/16–06/24/16).

36. We report the second visits that were started by the *Socii* and concluded with the presence of the Master: to the Province of Croatia (01/14/15–01/24/15), to the General Vicariate of the Democratic Republic of Congo (07/12/15–07/24/15), to the Province of St. Rose of Flanders and the Vice Province of St. Thomas Aquinas in Belgium (09/21/15–09/28/15), to the Province of The Most Holy Name of Jesus in the USA (10/20/15–11/03/15), to the Province of Austria and Upper Germany (11/25/15–11/29/15), to the Province of Toulouse (01/11/16–01/18/16), and to the Province of Poland (04/07/16–04/24/16).

37. We report that during the past three years, the Master of the Order made canonical visits made through delegates to the Vicariate of Trinidad (09/14/13–09/23/13), to the friars of the Province of England in Granada and Barbados (09/24/13–09/29/13), to the Province of Slovakia (10/02/13–10/09/13), to the General Vicariate of Taiwan (11/05/13–11/13/13), to the Convent of St. Mary Major in Rome (01/21/14–01/23/14), to the General Vicariate of South Africa (01/31/14–02/14/14), to the Vicariate St. Vincent Liem of the Vietnamese Province in North America (06/11/14–06/26/14), to Biblical School of Jerusalem (04/27/15–04/29/15), to the Vicariate of Angola of the Province of Portugal (06/01/15–06/01/15), and to the Vicariate of the Province of Canada in Japan (04/08/16–04/16/16).

38. We report that during the past three years, the Master of the Order made numerous fraternal visits and bequests to the celebration of the Jubilee of the Order and participated in various international meetings of friars and other members of the Dominican Family: visit to the St. Stephen's community of Jerusalem (04/16/14–04/20/14), to meeting IEOP in Dublin (04/23/14–04/25/14), to the Beatification of Br. Giuseppe Girotti (04/26/14), to the assembly of the European Laity Commission (05/25/14), to the meeting CIDALC in Cuba (06/02/14–06/05/14), to the meeting of the Spanish nuns (06/07/14), to the meeting of priors provincial of the Spanish provinces (07/01/14–07/02/14), to the meeting of priors provincial and vicars provincial in Rome (07/07/14–07/11/14), to the conference on philosophy and theology in Oakland, California (07/15/14–07/20/14), to the IAOP meeting in Kenya (07/21/14–07/24/14), to the General Chapter of the Sisters of the Presentation (07/25/14–07/28/14), the *Journées Romaines* on interreligious dialogue in Indonesia (08/12/14–08/16/14), to visit with the brothers and sisters in Iraq (10/23/14–10/24/14), celebration of St. Albert the Great in Freiburg (11/14/14 to 11/16/14), to the Eucharistic commemoration on the anniversary of the Belgian martyrs of the Congo in Brussels (11/22/14–11/23/14), to visit with the brothers and sisters in Bangui (03/31/15–04/08/15), the IEOP meeting in Madonna dell'Arco (04/09/15–04/10/15), to a conference in Toronto on Theology, the Dominicans and the Second Vatican Council (05/05/15–05/09/15), the Mass of Pentecost in Toulouse to open the Jubilee celebrations in France (05/23/15–05/24/15), to the meeting on various forms of consecrated life in Taizé (07/07/15–07/11/15), to a continuing education meeting with the sisters in Spain (08/12/15–08/13/15), to a meeting with the nuns of *Europa Utriusque* in Kraków (09/03/15–09/05/15), visiting the friars community in Albania (09/19/15–09/20/15), to a Jubilee congress about Father Lagrange (10/23/15–10/24/15), to Jubilee celebrations in Paris (12/11/15–12/13/15), to the opening of the new Province of Hispania (01/02/16–01/04/16), to a Jubilee congress in Zagreb on interreligious dialogue (01/08/16–01/10/16), CIDALC jubilee celebration in Bogotá (01/30/16), a Jubilee celebration in Paris (02/06/16–02/07/16), to an assembly of priestly fraternities (02/22/16–02/24/16), to a Jubilee congress on the word of God in the PUST (02/25/16–02/27/16), to an IEOP meeting in Dubrovnik (03/30/16–04/03/16), to a Jubilee celebration in London (04/29/16–04/30/16), to a Jubilee

celebration Lund (05/20/16–05/22/16), a Eucharist with the Dominican school of Vechta in Bologna (06/18/16), a Jubilee celebration in Paris (06/25/16–06/27/16), a pilgrimage, "In the Footsteps of St. Dominic," with the student brothers and sisters in formation (07/01/16–07/14/16), to a Dominican congress of educators in Spain (07/04/16).

39. We report that, since the last General Chapter, the Master of the Order has granted the degree of Master of Sacred Theology to: fr. Walter Senner and fr. Tiemo Rainer Peters of the Province of Teutonia, fr. Jan Andrzej Kłoczowski of the Province of Poland, fr. Hisao Miyamoto of the Province of Canada, and fr. Miguel Nunez de Burgos of the Province of Hispania.

40. We report that from July 7-11, 2014, a meeting of priors provincial and regional and provincial vicars was held at the Pontifical Angelicum University in Rome to discuss the restructuring of the Order.

41. We report that on November 7, 2015 in the Basilica of Santa Sabina, the Master of the Order in the presence of numerous major superiors and representatives of the Dominican Family, members of the General Curia and guests from different religious orders, celebrated the solemn opening of the jubilee year of the eight hundredth anniversary of the confirmation of the Order of Preachers.

42. We report that His Holiness Pope Francis received in a private audience the Master of the Order, fr. Bruno Cadoré, on September 9, 2013.

43. We report that the Master of the Order, fr. Bruno Cadoré, participated in the XIV Ordinary General Assembly of the Synod of Bishops, held in Rome October 4-25, 2015.

44. We report that on October 13, 2013, our brothers, fr. Raimundo Castaño and fr. José María González Solís, were beatified.

45. We report that on April 26, 2014, our brother, fr. Giuseppe Girotti, was beatified.

46. We report that on September 19, 2015, our brother, Monsiñor Pio Alberto del Corona, was beatified.

47. We report that on May 17, 2015, María Alfonsina Danil Ghattas, a Dominican tertiary, was canonized.

48. We report that during the last three years, His Holiness has appointed Monsignor Francisco Malcolm Patrick McMahon, Metropolitan Archbishop of Liverpool (England); Bishop Anthony Fisher, Metropolitan Archbishop of Sydney (Australia); Bishop Christopher Cardone, Archbishop of Honiara (Solomon Islands); fr. David Macaire, Archbishop of Fort-de-France; fr. Carlos Azpiroz Costa, coadjutor Archbishop of Bahia Blanca (Argentina); fr. Lorenzo Piretto, Archbishop of Izmir (Turkey); and fr. Roger Houngbedji, Archbishop of Cotonou (Benin).

49. We report that during the last three years, the Holy Father appointed fr. Jorge Angel Pedraza Saldias, Auxiliary Bishop of La Paz (Bolivia); fr. David Martinez de Aguirre Guinea to the title of the Apostolic Vicariate of Puerto Maldonado (Peru); and fr. Jorge Giovanny Pazmiño as Bishop of the Diocese of Ambato (Ecuador).

50. We report that on February 25, 2014, the Master of the Order, fr. Bruno Cadoré, was appointed a member of the Congregation for Institutes of Consecrated Life and Societies of Apostolic Life.

51. We report that from November 25-29, 2014, the Master of the Order, fr. Bruno Cadoré, participated in the Plenary Assembly of the Congregation for Institutes of Consecrated Life and Societies of Apostolic Life: "*New wine in new wine skins: Consecrated Life on the 50th Anniversary of* Perfectae Caritatis."

52. We report that fr. Gerard Timoner was appointed a member of the International Theological Commission.

53. We report that fr. Miroslav Konstanc Adam was appointed prelate auditor of the Apostolic Tribunal of the Roman Rota.

54. We report that His Holiness Pope Francis held an audience for the members of this General Chapter on August 4, 2016 (cf. Appendices II and III).

55. We report that the General Chapter concluded its work on August 4, the Solemnity of Our Holy Father Dominic, with a solemn con-celebrated Mass in the Basilica of San Domenico, Bologna. The Eucharist was presided over by Monsignor Matteo Maria Zuppi, Archbishop of Bologna. The homily was given by fr. Bruno Cadoré, Master of the Order.

Chapter II: Prologue

Sent to preach grace and mercy

56. In this General Chapter of Bologna, we began a new stage in our journey of itinerant preaching. We have started the Chapter sessions finding ourselves with young men in formation who had sojourned "In the Footsteps of St. Dominic," in the eighth centenary of the approval of the Order. This meeting has encouraged and challenged us. Together with them we wish to renew ourselves and to find new zeal in the place where our Father was reborn into eternal life. We ask him to accompany us in this task, thus fulfilling his promise "to be more useful to the brothers."

57. The providential coincidence of the *Jubilee of the Order* and the *Extraordinary Jubilee of Mercy* gives us the opportunity to reflect a new light on our life and mission as preachers. We are Dominicans by the grace of God. At the beginning of this path we were asked: "What do you seek? "And answered: "God's mercy and yours." From that moment our Dominican life began, overwhelmed by the goodness of God, and we exercise ministry of the Word as *misericordia veritatis* (the mercy of truth, cf. ACG Providence 2001 107). Pope Emeritus Benedict XVI reminds us that "There is no action more beneficial – and therefore more charitable – towards one's neighbor than to break the bread of the word of God, to share with him the Good News of the Gospel, to introduce him to a relationship with God," (Lenten message 2013, n. 3).

58. The ministry of the Word is, in fact, an act of charity, mercy, and generosity that drives us to share our greatest treasure, the Word made flesh. Truly, "the greatest work of charity is evangelization." To preach or to teach, nourished by assiduous study, is rightly seen as a work of charity and as an expression of our Dominican prophetic mission. Moreover, the corporal and spiritual works of mercy are a preaching because they proclaim the merciful love of God.

59. The Order, since its inception, has fulfilled this ministry, which has been none other than the mission to which we are called today: "we are sent to preach the Gospel." The last General Chapter pinpointed

what the questions are that will help us to renew (cf. ACG Trogir 2013 50 and 51).

60. In Bologna we remembered, as stated in Trogir, and we found that the preaching of the Order is marked by some fundamental points that sustain our vocation, give meaning to our lives, drive our mission, and invite us to share the Gospel with a suffering world. These points are indicated in the text of Luke 10: 1-20 when the disciples are sent out to preach, showing them who sent them [n.61-65], how they are sent [nn. 66-69], for what does He send them [70-73], where to send them [74-77], and what must be the fruit of being sent [78-81].

"The Lord appointed another seventy-two"

61. Who sends them? Having gathered the twelve and having sent them to preach the kingdom of God, the Lord appointed seventy-two others to perform the same task. Now He sends the whole Dominican Family to proclaim the Good News as witnesses of that kingdom and makes us sharers of the apostolic mission. We are sent to preach the Gospel to the men and women of our time with an ever new vitality.

62. Our sending is based on the trust that God has placed in the Order of Preachers. This continued confidence renews us at every historical moment in the Church and strengthens our friendship with the Lord; demands fidelity to listening to the Word; but it also requires a trusted encounter with the world, and responsibility and commitment to human situations of great vulnerability. As such, the demands of friendship in the preachers of grace renew the conversation with the world.

63. A conversation of friendship with God and with the world makes possible a more positive preaching and the discovery of God's grace in those around us; it puts more emphasis on the possibilities of human beings than on their limits; appreciates the human capacity for good and reconciliation; and thus expresses a certain complicity between God and the preacher.

64. St. Dominic sent his friars to study, to preach, and to found convents, showing great confidence in his brethren. These tasks show us that

life in community, study, and preaching are the foundations of our identity. We preach together when we pray together, grow in our fraternity, and study the Word.

65. The Order today takes up the challenge to renew its obedience to God and to His Word, which is incarnated in the world. For this renewal to be true, we need to hear the cries of humanity. Thus our preaching springs up not from ourselves but from a God who speaks to His people.

"He sent them two by two"

66. How are they sent? The Lord sends us, like the other seventy-two, two by two. He goes with us as He did with the disciples on the road to Emmaus. We are sent as a community, to share the mission of Dominic with countless brothers and sisters who have taken on itinerant preaching throughout the centuries across countries and continents. We are sent two by two on the same mission and from the same religious profession, some in the common priesthood and others in the exercise of the ministerial priesthood.

67. We have been sent as brothers to build communities. The fraternal and the contemplative life are part of our mission. For a Dominican, the witness of community life is something that can be difficult to achieve, but should be rewarding for us and uplifting for others. Fraternal life is constitutive of the identity of the preacher. The unanimity of heart and mind is an eloquent form of preaching because it lends credibility to the mission. How can we preach the love of God without building community with the brothers? ...because that is where we grow and mature in charity. For this reason, the Dominican community is called *sancta praedicatio* – the Holy Preaching.

68. Jesus, before sending them out two by two (Lk 10), had sent the twelve to proclaim the Kingdom and to bring salvation (Luke 9). The number of those sent may vary, and even the realities of those sent may change, but this does not alter the mission of preaching the truth in love (Eph 4: 15). What it requires is that we adapt our language to communicate the Word in dialogue with diverse peoples and cultures, and renew our structures to live in the midst of the changing conditions of today's world.

69. From the beginning we were conceived as a family, and this is how we are to fulfill today the task of preaching sustained by the prayers of our nuns, accompanied by the sisters of apostolic life, by the collaboration of the priestly and lay fraternities, by secular institutes and animated by the spirit of the members of the Dominican Youth Movement. During the Chapter we have shared the hopes and challenges of the various branches of our family, reaffirming our communion. Together we have creatively sought the best way to respond to our vocation.

"Heal the sick and say: The Kingdom of God is near"

70. For what does he send them? Jesus sends his disciples in mutual dependence with humanity; He says, "eat what is placed [before you]." Preachers are sent to share the bread of the Word, willing to take what they can give us; to feed on the Word and be fed by those we serve. This command of Jesus expresses a fragility. Here is the paradox of the preacher who experiences, on the one hand, the strength of the word of life that heals and uplifts and, on the other hand, the fragility of the means at his disposal to announce the weakness of his existence, even to relying on the benevolence of those who receive it. This vulnerability is where the preacher experiences the confidence that leads to the audacity of the sower of the Word. The mystique of the preacher is thus that of the sower. He plants and cares for what he sowed. Germination, growth and harvesting depend on the Lord of the harvest and constitute a marvelous mystery.

71. Second, Jesus lives and shares with His disciples, and then sends them to announce what they have lived and shared with Him, that is, the Kingdom. Called to the preaching, we have been invited to live with Him, to proclaim the Word, and to carry out His same actions. *Contemplare et aliis tradere* [to contemplate and to share with others] are the two poles of our lives. Announcing the nearness of the Kingdom of God and healing the sick brings us closer to the places where the harmony of human beings and our societies are broken. Where the poor and the little ones are, there God is. His presence prevents them from being forgotten and ignored. The preacher, a sign of hope and of the goodness of God, will be there to make God present. "In each of these 'little ones,' Christ himself is

present... His flesh becomes visible [anew]... to be acknowledged, touched, and cared for by us" (cf. *Misericordiae Vultus*, n. 15).

72. Third, we are sent to preach God's mercy and our reconciliation with Him and our brothers (cf. 2 Cor 5: 20). Dominican preaching, as with Dominic, must pacify wounded relationships and bring peace to the world. So we must understand that the preaching of mercy is a healing mission. Our way of preaching is a path of inner healing, a path of reconciliation in communities and in the provinces. In this way we praise, bless, and preach the Gospel of joy, peace, and reconciliation.

73. Finally, although our preaching should be healing, throughout history we have made mistakes that have hurt many people, including our own brothers. In this jubilee we need reconciliation with those whom we have hurt by our infidelities, arrogance, and excessive defense of non-critical issues.

"To the places (cities) where He must go"

74. Where does He send them? He sends them, "to the places where He should go." St. Dominic preached the Good News of the "Word made flesh" in times of confusion in faith and crisis in the Church. Today we live in a globalized world that shows various complex realities. There are places in the world mired in materialism, secularism, atheism, political polarization, unsupportive economic development, marginalization and indifference, individualism, social violence, racial discrimination, and threats to the institution of marriage and the family. In other places, people live in extreme poverty, under the violence of war, abuse of human rights with impunity, religious fundamentalism, terrorism and corruption. All this causes anxiety and despair.

75. Our preaching is contextualized not only in the places where we are, but also in the people who inhabit them; in men and women who need the announcement of hope founded in Christ. Therefore, in this General Chapter, the Order is committed to migrants and displaced persons; to indigenous peoples; to those who profess another religion, to those belonging to other Christian churches or are indifferent to faith; to the forgotten; to the unborn, the young, and the elderly; to the sick, prisoners, death row inmates, etc. This leads

us to renew our commitment to life, to education, to human development, to campus ministry, to parish ministry, and to health care.

76. Today the Order is sent to preach in the "digital world," a reality which also needs to be evangelized. Technological advances offer us a powerful tool for preaching. The internet and social networks have become a new pulpit that assists us in our preaching and encourages dialogue and interaction in a polarized and divided society.

77. Our preaching, motivated by mercy, cannot ignore reconciliation between humanity and creation. Global ecological changes have advanced rapidly in recent decades, affecting the poorest and most vulnerable. One must grow in sensitivity to this challenge. Pope Francis, in his encyclical, *Laudato Si*, calls for responsible action with the earth and the need for an "ecological balance" for the common good.

"They returned full of joy"

78. What must be the fruit of being sent? The disciples returned full of joy after completing their mission. In this jubilee year there are many reasons for joy in the Order. We thank God for them because its mission is still valid; because God opens new scenarios for preaching; because we are blessed with the vocations of those who are already in the Order and also with those who are becoming a part of our family.

79. The disciples return full of joy knowing that preaching is not a simple announcement, but a paschal commitment: to die to oneself in order to announce life. The preacher is giving life in his journey. Some in situations of violence and rejection; others in silence, in Easter testimony, striving daily to be faithful to their vocation; and some members of our family, in more sublime ways, also have shed their blood throughout history, like fr. Pierre Claverie, O.P., who was killed twenty years ago in serving the Gospel in the midst of a fragmented society. However, these groups were overjoyed because they realized that the "value" of life lies in the ability to give it for others.

80. On the preaching journey all is not easy. "There is a lot of dust in the preacher's sandals which must be shaken off." We must let go of individualism, infidelities, lack of identity, fear, and self-referentiality, lest we forget that we are servants of a common mission. Clinging to positions, places and communities, or to prefer-ence for traditional ministries and less creativity can reduce our boldness in preaching. As we noted above, the preaching journey is not all favorable, and this can result in negative attitudes or discouragement which should be shed. "Shaking [the dust from] our sandals" is important so that nothing tarnishes our joy.

81. The joy of the disciples is not so much what they have done for themselves as much as their having served humanity "in the name of Jesus." Returning as disciples to the side of the Master is not to forget the world, but to share with Jesus the wounds of the people. This is what Dominic did: "after speaking of God to men, he spoke with God about men." Taking the path back to God is to refocus our lives on the One who sent us. This is *vera laetitia praedicatoris [the true joy of the preacher]*.

"Nothing can harm them. Their names are written in heaven"

82. St. Dominic left no written homily. From him we only have few writings, but all his life is a sermon, and the Order he founded is his best homily. Dominicans today must feel a part of this *praedicatio [preaching]* of St. Dominic, because we are the words with which he continues to preach in history.

83. The first General Chapter of the Order was held in Bologna; right here, as we celebrate the eighth centenary, we acknowledge with grateful memory the action of the Spirit and invoke the provident grace and mercy of God to continue the mission to which we have been called.

84. The future presents us with many challenges and tasks. However, the Order renews its trust in God and its hope in the commitment of the brothers, especially the younger ones, because we are aware that we have a great story to tell and a great future to build. Therefore, in this Jubilee we are again sent to praise, to bless and to preach.

Chapter III: Apostolic Creativity

A Spirituality of Listening

85. [Declaration] Aware of and attentive to the SIGNS OF THE TIMES, Dominicans find themselves in permanent dialogue with the Word of God, the Church, the People of God, the Order, and the Dominican Family, as well as with a broad spectrum of other religions and cultures. Being "in dialogue" means listening as well as speaking. We are challenged to remain open to the truth of the other in every dialogue.

86. [Exhortation] We exhort all members of the Order to reflect on Pope Francis' words to the Conclave before his election that the greatest evil that over time can befall the Church is that of self-referentiality, a type of theological narcissism which tempts the Church to believe and act as though its light comes from itself and not from Christ.

87. [Commendation] We recommend that all members of the Order reflect on listening toward dialogue in preaching – a listening that is humble, patient, empathetic, reasonable, critical, merciful and compassionate, practical and discerning – a listening that is open to the truth of the other.

88. [Commendation] In the hope of improving fraternal communication within our communities and contributing positively through our preaching to the level of discourse in today's society, we recommend that promoters of permanent formation encourage communities to study the art of debate (*disputatio*) in Dominican life and to participate in lectures and discussions on this topic outside our immediate priories and houses whenever possible.

89. [Commendation] We recommend discussion among all our communities of what it means to move from an acknowledgement of diversity to that of "Reconciled Diversity." We also recommend that superiors seek new ways of fostering communication among the brethren, especially among those who are divided over ecclesiological differences and conflicts.

90. [Commendation] We recommend that priors provincial, vice-provincials and vicars provincial organize times of reflection on the Word of God, study and analysis of social realities and the principal

challenges of the local churches, in preparation for their Chapters and assemblies.

Care of Creation

91. [Declaration] Global ecological changes in the world today call for radical changes in styles of life and in modern practices of production and consumption. Concern for nature is inseparable from justice for the most vulnerable, social commitment, and interior peace. With this in mind, we should give particular attention to the presence of vast amounts of the byproducts of human technology, such as radioactive nuclear waste.

In the dialogues between Jesus and His disciples, we note His invitation to recognize the relationship that God, as Father, has with all His creatures, recalling with great tenderness that none of His creatures is alien or far from Him.

92. [Exhortation] We exhort the priors provincial and their councils to include complementary environmental studies in their *Ratio Studiorum Particularis* programs, bearing in mind the distinct levels of "ecological equilibrium" indicated in the Encyclical, *Laudato Si:* internal equilibrium within oneself, equilibrium in solidarity with others, natural equilibrium with other beings, and spiritual equilibrium with God.

93. [Exhortation] We exhort priors and superiors to include an environmental impact analysis of the lifestyle of their communities while organizing the community projects.

Mission renewal

94. [Declaration] All brothers listen to the Word of God in order to hear the cries and suffering of the People of God. This listening should inspire the direction and implementation of their apostolic activities.

Migration

95. [Declaration] Migration has reached a dramatic height today. Many countries have closed their borders, even when the right to asylum is most evident.

96. [Thanksgiving] We thank the communities in the Order who have welcomed refugees.

97. [Exhortation] We exhort all our communities to welcome and support refugees according to their resources and abilities.

Indigenous Peoples

98. [Declaration] In many parts of the world, indigenous peoples have preserved their traditions, thanks to the vital force, which emanates from their ancestral human and communitarian values. However, today they are subject to social, political, economic, cultural, and religious forces that menace their existence and well-being.

99. [Exhortation] Following the compassion of St. Dominic, we exhort the brothers to contribute to the preservation of indigenous peoples through solidarity with them and the preaching of the Gospel of Jesus Christ.

Interreligious Dialogue

100. [Declaration] We note with concern the growth of fundamentalism, the increase of fear and violence in different parts of the world.

101. [Declaration] New developments within the Muslim world challenge our mission. We encourage those communities who are living and working among strong Muslim majorities. We thank them for their witness. Their experiences, which should be known and appreciated among the whole Dominican family, demonstrate in a credible way how we can exercise our mission in a "plural humanity" (Pierre Claverie, O.P.), learn from the culture and the religion of the other, and engage in constructive dialogue.

102. [Thanksgiving] We thank the friars at IDEO (Dominican Institute for Oriental Studies) for their outstanding work in the field of dialogue between Islam and Christianity and for their program in Islamic studies for Dominicans in formation. We also thank the Peace Center of Lahore.

103. [Commendation] We recommend that provinces consider sending friars to Cairo to participate in the program of formation that IDEO offers. We further recommend that friars already formed in Islamic

studies share their knowledge and experiences with their provinces when opportune, e.g. at study days, provincial assemblies and/or other events.

104. [Commendation] Aware of the importance, both historically and in the present, of the Dominican presence in Turkey, we recommend that the Master of the Order support and assist the prior provincial of St. Dominic in Italy and his Council to specify objectives, needs and opportunities for ministry, in pursuit of the collaboration necessary for a continuing, sustainable Dominican presence.

105. [Declaration] During the 2016 General Chapter at Bologna, the capitulars honored the twentieth anniversary of the death of our brother, Pierre Claverie, O.P., Bishop of Oran, Algeria, who was assassinated on the first day of August, 1996.

Knowing that his cause of beatification, along with eighteen other martyrs of the church of Algeria, has been opened by the Diocese of Algiers, the Chapter wishes to express our profound gratitude for the witness of our brother, wishing to embrace his example and commitment to "plural humanity." At this moment in our own history, we are honored to offer our prayerful support of his cause for beatification.

Apostolate in City Centers

106. [Declaration] The General Chapter at Trogir spoke of ministry in city centers: "to offer places of listening and meeting for those who are lonely and abandoned, as well as those who don't normally come to our churches," (ACG Trogir 2013 111 §4). Given sociological realities of many cities today, the economically disadvantaged are often forced out of city centers and into the peripheries. This can eventually eliminate entire social classes.

107. [Exhortation] We exhort communities who have been entrusted with a church, parish, or cultural center to remain attentive to the diversity of the public to which they direct themselves, so that their preaching of charity reaches everyone, including the most disadvantaged. This can be done in different ways: by organizing conferences about economic and social realities and by participating in various acts of solidarity.

Dominican Ministry Centers

108. [Declaration] Friars Preachers face many challenges today, such as diminished numbers, a lack of common mission, excessive individualism, to name just a few. Nevertheless, in this 800th Jubilee year, we believe that we are equipped to renew ourselves for the future, given recommendations of recent Chapters for broader collaboration in ministry, and aware of current considerations of restructuring so as to foster healthier community life.

109. [Declaration] Many of our convents have been and still are today significant Dominican centers, from which a wider breadth of ministries flows within the context of community life. Such models can serve us equally well today. As centers (or hubs) for Dominican apostolate, they can offer a wide variety of ministries, allow for greater Dominican family collaboration, and contribute to the ongoing renewal of common life and the community project.

110. [Commendation] Acknowledging that some larger ministry sites of this sort already exist, we recommend that priors provincial and their councils strengthen those communities in whatever ways possible and consider the establishment of additional such centers. New establishments of this type could require closures of other, possibly smaller, missions.

111. [Commendation] We recommend that provinces and vice provinces work together in the establishment of such centers, broadening out to the possibility of creating international centers, and that they invite the collaboration of other branches of the Dominican family.

The Rosary and Pilgrimages

112. [Declaration] The Rosary is an important apostolic medium, which draws together people from many backgrounds. It is also a precious instrument for people in situations of great suffering (illness, prison, exile, etc.).

113. [Commendation] We recommend that provincial promoters of the Rosary creatively renew the Rosary apostolate, through modern

means of communication, collaborating with the Dominican family and involving younger brothers.

Parish Ministry

114. [Declaration] Bishops entrust parishes to provinces and vice provinces to take advantage of the Order's preaching charism. Although pastors are named, this apostolate ought to be assumed in a communitarian manner.

115. [Exhortation] We exhort friars who work in parishes to listen carefully to the needs of the faithful, to facilitate Christian fraternity, and to work towards solidarity and parish unity, all in service of the Gospel.

Education and Evangelization

116. [Declaration] The teaching apostolate is a privileged place for contact with younger generations who will assume responsibilities in society, in the midst of realities that promote impoverishment and the exclusion of persons. Faced with situations of violence, terrorism, fundamentalism, forced migration, the lack of recognition of personal dignity and the destruction of human values, evangelization and accompaniment of students is necessary.

117. [Exhortation] We exhort brothers engaged in pastoral ministry to students and in universities to encourage reflection among the students themselves on current realities and to promote formation in Christian values based on *misericordia veritatis*, the mercy of truth (cf. ACG Providence 2001 Ch. III, Prol. 107).

118. [Exhortation] We encourage provinces and vice provinces to continue the development of the Salamanca Process, as the Chapter of Trogir requested (cf. ACG Trogir 2013 112-113).

Study as a Mission of the Order

119. [Declaration] In the Order of Preachers, preaching of the truth is the apostolic goal of all study. Therefore, the Order requires excellent academic programs for the proper fulfilment of its mission.

120. [Commendation] We recommend that priors provincial and regents of study encourage friars in formation for biblical studies to utilize the resources offered by the École Biblique in Jerusalem, such as preparation for exams with the Biblical Commission, doctorates and summer courses.

121. [Commendation] We recommend that provinces, which have not already done so, establish preaching workshops that include experiences that offer a preaching more tailored to the necessities and demands of the modern world, such as *Retraite dans la ville, GodzDogz.*

Prison and Health Care Apostolate

122. [Declaration] A considerable number of friars work in prison and health care ministries. They accompany those who are going through these difficult situations and their families. This apostolate is realized at the frontiers of life and death.

123. [Exhortation] We exhort other friars in community with these brothers to support them in these particular ministries.

124. [Thanksgiving] We thank all friars called to preach in prison and hospital ministries for the hope and companionship they bring.

Common project

125. [Declaration] The celebration of the Jubilee of the Order helps us widen our capacity to listen to the Word of God, and, therefore, to see in a new way the human reality which cries out for life, truth and mercy.

126. [Commendation] We recommend that all brothers study once again the letter of the Master of the Order on the community project. We recommend further that all house lectors conduct meetings on the understanding and promotion of the community project, seeking new conversations, new ideas, new energy, new life and renewed commitment.

Foundations

127. [Commendation] Given our ongoing commitment to the universal mission of the Order, we recommend that the following criteria be employed by the Master and his Council in preparation for establishing new foundations:

1) careful study of the needs of both the people to be served and the local church;
2) awareness of and sensitivity to local culture, customs and language, as well as of societal and political realities of the region;
3) preparedness for both short and long term financial and human resource needs.

128. [Commendation] The creativity needed to establish new foundations requires a similar creativity when withdrawing from ministries. It is often necessary to close missions in order to open new ones. This demands sensitivity. We recommend that the following criteria be employed in this process:

1) inclusion of the local Dominican community members in the discernment process and provision of opportunities for emotional and psychological assistance to brothers, if deemed necessary;
2) consultation and dialogue with the local church authority and sensitive communication of our decision to the people we serve who are affected by such decisions;
3) clear awareness of and regard for contractual obligations (ecclesial or civil) which may be involved;
4) ongoing analysis (both for and against) throughout the process of closing a foundation;
5) clarity and steadfastness in the decision, once it is made.

Cooperator Brothers

129. [Exhortation] Taking into account the important role of Cooperator Brothers in our Order and the ongoing need of a consistent and creative way of living the vocation of a preacher, we exhort priors provincial, vice-provincials and formators to promote

a model that implies three well-balanced foundations in which the brothers are engaged:

1) Contemplation. Cooperator brothers, through their religious consecration, are called to a profound relationship with God. It is essential that every brother recognizes his uniquely characteristic gift of contemplation and that it guides him to know God and to preach boldly in witness of his love.

2) Preaching and Study. In light of the teachings of the Second Vatican Council, the Dominican Cooperator Brothers' study of 2013 and in full support of a healthy self-identity, we encourage Cooperator Brothers to understand their vocation as fully integrated into the mainstream of the common preaching, with full access to and opportunity for permanent study.

3) Service. In recent times, the vocation of the Cooperator Brother has expanded to include new forms of service, witness and preaching. We encourage formators, superiors and promoters of permanent formation to support and assist Cooperator Brothers in maintaining balance between the demands for traditional forms of service and opportunities for new ministries.

Promotion of the Dominican Family

130. [Declaration] We note and rejoice in the fact that in many places around the world "the Dominican Family (which) is composed of clerical and cooperator brothers, nuns, sisters, members of secular institutes and fraternities of priests and laity" (LCO 9) works together in common apostolic projects.

131. [Exhortation] We exhort priors provincial to initiate in their territories a meeting of the superiors or representatives of each branch of the Dominican family, so as to establish a working group to discern the possibility of accepting a common mission in real and practical ways and, where necessary, to develop statutes to guide the relationship in the common mission.

132. [Exhortation] We exhort priors provincial to promote communication throughout the Dominican family and to establish methods and procedures to facilitate a continuous dialogue among us.

133. [Exhortation] We exhort priors provincial, vice-provincials and vicars provincial to ensure the participation of members of the Dominican family during the preparation and celebration of their respective chapters.

134. [Exhortation] Given the unique role of the nuns in the preaching mission of the Order, we exhort all members of the Dominican family to provide material and spiritual support to the nuns' monasteries, especially those on the margins of society.

135. [Commendation] We recommend that those responsible for the Dominican laity assist in their formation when requested.

136. [Commendation] We recommend priors provincial, vice-provincials and formators to promote full understanding of and disposition towards the universal mission of the Order in all stages of formation.

137. [Exhortation] Given the Decree on the Laity of the Second Vatican Council, we exhort the Dominican laity, IDYM and DVI to create opportunities of honest dialogue with those who are unchurched, indifferent or alienated from the Church.

138. [Exhortation] We exhort our communities to foster the apostolates of IDYM and, through adequate formation, to integrate them as partners in our preaching.

139. [Exhortation] We exhort communities accompanying youth groups to encourage their integration into IDYM.

140. [Commendation] We recommend that the Promoter for Dominican Laity assist DVI in developing new guidelines to help revive DVI, taking into account its positive contributions to the Mission of the Order.

141. [Thanksgiving] The Order recognizes and appreciates the presence and enriching witness of the Secular Institutes within the mission of the Order. We thank the members of the Dominican Secular Institutes for their witness of life and preaching, through which they affirm the presence and mercy of God in daily life.

Contemporary World

Faith and Science

142. [Declaration] Often, faith and the sciences are viewed as being in conflict. Likewise, faith can be deemed obsolete. Our brother, St. Thomas Aquinas, wrote: "the light of reason and the light of faith both proceed from God," (*Summa contra Gentiles* 1, 7). In this we recognize the necessity of entering into an authentic and productive dialogue with the sciences.

143. [Exhortation] We exhort regents of study and masters of students to encourage students in initial formation to explore and discern a ministry of study which promotes commitment to and dialogue between faith and science.

144. [Commendation] We recommend that our study centers organize workshops, presentations or colloquia that foster dialogue between scientists and theologians.

Dialogue with Indifference

145. [Declaration] St. Dominic listened attentively to the realities surrounding his life. In establishing the Order, he combined religious traditions of the past with new practices adopted from the new evangelical movements of his time, out of which he proclaimed the Gospel.

146. [Exhortation] We exhort the brethren that, in proclaiming the Word of God and through the witness of their lives, they combine centuries of church tradition with knowledge of the wisdom of the children of this world, allowing themselves to be inspired by whatever is worthy in contemporary social, economic and political life; in the practices of different Christian communities; among believers of other religions; and even among those who make themselves enemies of God and of the Church.

147. [Declaration] In his apostolic exhortation *Evangelii Gaudium*, Pope Francis encourages us to cultivate special meeting places in "new Areopagi," like the "Court of the Gentiles," where "believers and non-believers, are able to engage in dialogue about fundamental issues of ethics, art and science, and about the search for transcendence" (*Evangelii Gaudium*, 257). As the Order of

Preachers we have a rich tradition in creating such meeting places; however, the "culture of indifference," which does not wish to dialogue, challenges us.

148. [Exhortation] We exhort priors provincial and their councils, in preparing for the next General Chapter, to produce a serious reflection, in an interesting and practical way, on how the friars can engage the culture of indifference.

149. [Exhortation] We exhort our brothers involved in local pastoral ministries to examine and discern, along with members of the Dominican family, how to dialogue with the culture of indifference and to reflect on ways to develop a joint pastoral strategy.

150. [Commendation] Considering the possibility that Acts of provincial chapters over the next two years might address the "Culture of Indifference," we recommend that after approval of the various Acts, the Master of the Order and his Council consider offering a summary report of this topic to share with the Order.

Digital Continent

151. [Declaration] The vertiginous development of electronic communications media in our contemporary world presents us with new virtual frontiers, which include social networks and other forms of social interaction by means of digital media. Pope Emeritus Benedict XVI has called this the "digital continent." It represents more than three billion people connected to the internet.

This information explosion provides twenty-first-century Dominicans with a new pulpit, allowing us to bring the Gospel to people often beyond our reach, as well as advancing causes, such as justice and peace, which are rooted in our foundational charism.

152. [Commendation] We recommend to priors provincial, vice-provincials and vicars provincial that they explore and promote the proper use of the virtual world (internet) as an instrument for listening to the tendencies and social necessities of our times, and as a tool for preaching. It can also be valuable in establishing community projects.

153. [Exhortation] We exhort provinces and vice provinces to promote the formation of friars in order to enable them to face this new challenge of preaching, drawing, if necessary, on the regional and international resources of the Order.

154. [Commendation] Disruptive technologies are also transforming our societies and economies in wholly new and extremely rapid ways. They have a powerful impact in the field of Catholic social teaching and challenge our Christian anthropology. Some Dominican initiatives like the think-tank, OPTIC (Order of Preachers for Technology, Information, and Communication), have already engaged at a certain level with the developers of these technologies. We recommend that the Master of the Order foster support of these existing initiatives, especially by encouraging the development of local projects stemming from them, and by actively soliciting the involvement of both friars and the institutions of the Order.

155. [Commendation] For this purpose, we recommend that the Socius for the Intellectual Life write a letter to all regents of study asking them to identify friars and other scholars able to be involved in a reflection on digital technologies.

156. [Declaration] We further declare it important to acknowledge that the phenomenon of "virtual reality" can negatively influence people, especially the young, causing them to lose sensibility to religious symbolism and reality.

Promotion of Mission Networks

157. [Declaration] A digital platform called "Atrium" was established to create networks of friars (called: mission networks) working in particular apostolates. This allows friars involved in the same apostolic field to share best practices and to build common projects.

158. [Exhortation] In order to enable these mission networks to be effective on the larger scale, we exhort each province to appoint a friar, e.g. the provincial promoter for communication or the secretary of the province, to coordinate and promote them. He will have to: identify friars working in the relevant apostolic areas as

listed by the General Chapter of Trogir and promote their involvement in these mission networks; identify other groups of friars who could benefit from having a mission network on Atrium, both at the provincial and the regional levels; and assist them to identify goals and leaders; encourage all friars to use Atrium.

159. [Commendation] We recommend that the Master of the Order strengthen the technical team of the Promoter for Communications by appointing a technician to supervise the development of the mission networks.

160. [Commendation] We recommend that the Socius for Apostolic Life and the Promoter of Communications use the Mission Congress in Rome as an opportunity to develop mission networks.

Chapter IV: Restructuring and Collaboration

Restructuring

161. [Declaration] We declare that the process of restructuring of the Order into provinces, vice provinces and provincial vicariates initiated at the Rome Chapter (ACG Rome 2010 201-209) and approved at the Trogir Chapter (ACG Trogir 2013 154-161) is completed.

162. [Commission] We commission the Master of the Order to direct his socii or specific provinces to assist the new entities which have emerged to develop the structures necessary for them to realize their autonomy as vice provinces.

163. [Congratulation] We congratulate all the entities involved in this process of restructuring. We acknowledge that it has sometimes been difficult and painful for some brothers, and recognize all the efforts made throughout the last six years. We thank those entities that have united with one another. We also thank the provinces and vice provinces that have accepted provincial vicariates or houses and priories outside the territory of their own entities.

164. [Commission] We commission the Master to complete the restructuring of the Order. We declare that the General Vicariates of Taiwan and of South Africa are now established as vice provinces. We commission the Master of the Order to set up a process of accompaniment, of collaboration, and of evaluation of the consolidation of the two entities. He is also to present the state of their evolution to the General Council once a year. In like manner, concerning the General Vicariate of Chile, we commission the Master to accompany the process begun with the Province of Argentina according to LCO 256 bis. This process should be completed before the end of the year 2016. Until then, we declare that the norms for vice provinces not fulfilling the requirements of LCO 257 § I, shall be applied.

165. [Commission] Considering the fact that provinces and vice provinces have the same rights and obligations (LCO 257 § I,2) with the exception of their representation at an elective chapter, we commission the Master of the Order to review whether

retaining both kinds of entities is necessary for the sake of the mission of the Order.

166. [Inchoation] Considering that our life is conventual and for the sake of the mission, we initiate the following change in LCO 253 § I:

> 253. Const. § I. – A province consists of at least three convents, two of which must contain at least ~~ten~~ *eight* vocals. Furthermore, all the vocals of the province shall number at least forty.

167. [Commendation] We recommend that every provincial chapter should consider the proportion of its friars living in convents and houses in order to keep the unity of the friars, the Order's democratic ethos and the importance of the common mission.

168. [Ordination] Considering the fact that the assignation according to LCO 391, 6° has been both successful and difficult in differing places, times and circumstances, we ordain that such an assignation should only be done for specific reasons to assist in our preaching mission and for a definite term of not more than five years, subject to review and possible renewal.

Provincial Vicariates

169. [Recommendation] We recommend that the provincial vicariates of CIDALC build up relations with other provinces of the area to ensure that their intellectual and apostolic needs are met.

170. [Exhortation] We exhort the five provinces already involved in the Caribbean to reinforce their presence and contribute further to the life of the area.

Study

171. [Ordination] Following the orientations of the General Chapters of Rome (ACG Rome 2010 89-91) and Trogir (ACG Trogir 2013 85) to promote collaboration, we ordain the Socius for the Intellectual Life to organize with the coordinator of regents a meeting of regents in each region before the next General Chapter.

172. [Exhortation] We exhort the provincials and regents to identify and prepare future teachers with doctorates for the centers of institutional studies as well as the academic centers under the immediate jurisdiction of the Master of the Order. This exhortation is made in light of the urgent need for well-qualified teachers (ACG Rome 2010 86,107).

173. [Exhortation] We exhort provincials and regents to strengthen the philosophy program in the institutional formation of our brothers, one that will be academically rigorous in its presentation of ancient, scholastic and modern philosophy, and that will provide our students with an intellectual framework for further studies and apostolic work.

174. [Commendation] We recommend that the Master of the Order assist the provinces of Asia-Pacific to proceed with the proposal made by the regents and provincials of this region at their meeting in Ho Chi Minh City in February 2015 to establish a collaborative center of specialized study in Asia, the purpose of which would be to promote inter-religious dialogue between Christianity and the great religions of Asia, especially Hinduism, Buddhism, Confucianism, and Islam.

175. [Exhortation] We exhort the Socius for the Intellectual Life and the Socius for Apostolic Life to develop and strengthen intellectual initiatives in China for the sake of the mission there.

Institutions & Convents Under the Immediate Jurisdiction of the Master

176. [Commendation] We recommend that the rector of PUST organize, in strict collaboration with the other institutions under the immediate jurisdiction of the Master of the Order, and possibly in collaboration with other institutions such as IDEO, a course every two years in permanent formation for Dominicans and non-Dominicans, on topics in Dominican theology and spirituality. This course is to be held at PUST. The program should be financially self-sustaining, i.e., through course fees, travel as well as room and board paid by the course participants.

177. [Ordination] We ordain that professors at the PUST and the École Biblique receive an academic evaluation every five years by their proper academic authority. In addition, contracts for Dominican and non-Dominican professors in the institutions under the immediate jurisdiction of the Master of the Order are required. The contracts are to include a clear list of duties and obligations, which the professor is to fulfil, as is already done at the Theology Faculty at Fribourg. This list of duties and obligations should serve as a basis for evaluation.

178. [Ordination] We ordain that the rector of the PUST and its academic authorities review the current status of the Institute of St. Thomas Aquinas (which is part of PUST) and to decide upon its continuation or suppression.

179. [Commission] We commission the Master of the Order to request from the Congregation for Catholic Education the abrogation of the statutes of the *Convitto Internazionale san Tommaso d'Aquino* in Rome, so that it may become a residence for lay students, religious and priests who study at the PUST.

180. [Thanksgiving] We thank the friars assigned to the *Convitto Internazionale san Tommaso d'Aquino*, fr. Luke Buckles, OP (rector), fr. Paul Murray, OP (spiritual director), and fr. Albert Glade, OP (syndic), for their outstanding and continuing service.

181. [Commission] We commission the Master of the Order and his Socius for the Intellectual Life to explore the possibility of establishing a studentate for English-speaking student friars in Rome, so that they may pursue their institutional formation at the PUST.

182. [Recommendation] We recommend that the PUST appoint a director of development and fundraising. We invite both the PUST and the École Biblique to make their fundraising programs more professional in character.

183. [Commission] We commission the rector of PUST to form a committee to review the current statutes of the university (statutes approved *ad experimentum*), with the view to modifications,

including the possibility of a greater representation of the university's academic authorities on the *consiglio di amministrazione* (board of trustees). Such increased representation could improve communication between the board and the university's members.

184. [Ordination] We ordain that the rector of the PUST, the director of the École Biblique and the Prior of the Albertinum, after consultation with the Dean of the Faculty of Theology of the University of Fribourg, present to the Socius for the Intellectual Life a list of the faculty positions that must be filled within the next five years, with an indication of the precise qualifications needed for each position. The socius will then communicate this information to the provincials and regents of study.

185. [Exhortation] Following the orientations of the General Chapter of Trogir (ACG Trogir 2013 99), we exhort the institutions under the immediate jurisdiction of the Master to strengthen their relationships with the provinces, especially by contacts with provincials and regents of study, to collaborate more closely, so as to strengthen the faculties of these institutions.

186. [Commission] We commission the Master of the Order to establish an institute under his immediate jurisdiction in Africa. The institute should promote dialogue between theology, the different cultures of Africa, and its diverse traditional religions.

187. [Exhortation] We exhort the brethren teaching in Fribourg to continue and deepen their dialogue with other academic disciplines, such as international law, economics and medicine, at the university.

188. [Commission] We commission the Master of the Order to appoint a vicar who will have direct responsibility for the convents under the immediate jurisdiction of the Master.

Collaboration

189. [Declaration] In recognition that in our preaching mission in the contemporary world we do not have the resources or expertise to carry out on our own all the projects we would like to promote, we should collaborate with members of other branches of the

Dominican family and those outside the Dominican family as this becomes appropriate. Such acts of collaboration are to be welcomed as not merely necessary but as enriching for all those involved.

190. [Commendation] We recommend that the brothers promote different ways in which the different members of the Dominican family and others can participate in the projects of the provinces, as well as explore new initiatives which may be established by different branches of the Dominican family together.

191. [Ordination] We ordain that each province identify and support at least one interprovincial collaboration.

192. [Recommendation] We recommend that provinces explore ways in which interprovincial collaboration may occur in the areas of formation and study.

193. [Exhortation] We exhort provinces entering into interprovincial collaboration to recognize the challenges involved in sustaining such projects and the need to have a commitment to sustaining them in the longer term.

194. [Ordination] We ordain that when an interprovincial collaboration is proposed a clear plan be developed which sets out how the collaboration will be supported and what its timeline will be. The act of collaboration proposed should be set out in writing and state the reasons for the project, the responsibilities of those involved, how the project is to be supported financially, and how long the project is to run. This plan must be agreed to by the respective provincial councils and other appropriate bodies before it is executed. A written agreement must be signed and kept in the records of the provinces and other bodies involved.

195. [Exhortation] We urge the provinces of Hispania and San Juan Bautista of Peru to continue the process, and advance the fusion of the Provincial Vicariate "Santa Rosa" to the Province of Peru within the deadlines set by both entities. At the same time, we encourage to provinces and vice provinces in coordination with the priors provincial of Hispania and San Juan Bautista, to encourage the availability of some friars who can strengthen the apostolic

mission in the Amazon jungle, to ensure the presence of the Order to the indigenous peoples of the Peruvian Amazon.

Dominican Volunteers International (DVI)

196. [Commission] We commission the Master of the Order to seek a coordinator of the Dominican Volunteers International.

197. [Commission] We commission the coordinator of DVI to carry out a review of its activities in sending young people on placements in order to ensure that good and effective practice be identified for the future of the project. This review is to be submitted for approval to the DSI International Coordinator and the Promoter of the Laity.

198. [Commendation] We recommend that brothers involved in Dominican volunteer projects collaborate with the coordinator of DVI.

199. [Congratulation] We congratulate the brothers of the Province of France for establishing Dom&Go.

International Dominican Youth Movement (IDYM)

200. [Congratulation] We congratulate the International Dominican Youth Movement for its work to foster the mission of the Order among young people around the world in partnership with the branches of the Dominican family and to live out the charism of the Order in its organization and activities.

201. [Ordination] We ordain that in those provinces where the movement is present, following the statutes approved by the Master of the Order, the prior provincial appoint a brother to act as promoter of IDYM and that that brother work with local entities of the movement and with other members of the Dominican family to ensure that their formation and spiritual needs are met and to help the movement realize its mission.

202. [Recommendation] We recommend that where the movement is present a representative of IDYM be made a full member of any local or regional council of the Dominican Family.

Communications

203. [Thanksgiving] We thank those brothers in the different provinces who have worked in recent years to engage with the new forms of social media in order to promote the Order's mission within the new forms of communication found in the contemporary world.

204. [Commission] We commission the Promoter of Communications to form a team with three provincial promoters of communications to collaborate especially in ensuring the effective management of the Order's website.

Chapter V: The Life of the Brethren
Common Life and Government

From Brotherhood to Mission

205. [Declaration] Our life, following in Christ's footsteps in the way of St. Dominic, is a life of contemplation of the Word of God and of apostolic brotherhood, which is accomplished in each community with its gifts and weaknesses. This life is rooted in obedience to the apostolic outreach and in the communal undertaking of this mission, which before anything else presupposes the sharing of our expectations, of our charisms, of our personal abilities and material possessions.

206. [Exhortation] This apostolic brotherhood comes about thanks to the community project, the effective and realistic development of which must take into account the following prerequisites:

   1) Solidarity, based upon a recognition of everyone's needs and gifts, which is a fundamental characteristic of a fraternal and apostolic community. The community project must thus embody a commitment to communion and concern for the salvation of souls.
   2) Subsidiarity, as a means of growth in responsibility, which is necessary if our fraternal life and our apostolic mission are to exhibit responsible freedom. To this end, the community project must promote the charisms and the potentialities of each.
   3) Democracy, as an instrument of participative community government.

   These three preconditions should not only prevent the community from closing in upon itself, but should also promote a community project which guarantees a creative apostolic vitality.

Instruments for an effective community project.

207. [Declaration] Successive general chapters – beginning with Oakland (1989), which introduced the term "community project," and extending through the Letter of the Master of the Order (September, 2015) – have returned again and again to the necessity of community projects, recalling as during the Mexico

City Chapter that they are a way to positively channel the tension between common life and mission (ACG Mexico 1992 39; ACG Caleruega 1995 44; ACG Bologna 1998 127-132). Indeed, the community project is a good way to incorporate both solidarity and dialogue, and to facilitate both obedience and the exercise of the prior's authority, given the fact that even brothers working in different sectors can combine their efforts in striving to accomplish a community project which they have drawn up together.

208. [Declaration] Despite insistence upon the importance of the community project, the idea has not been sufficiently integrated into the lives of the brethren and the communities. This is primarily because the Acts of Chapters both general and provincial, as well as the Letters of the Master of the Order, have not been sufficiently well heeded. There is an obvious deficiency in the reception and in the contextual reading of these documents.

209. [Ordination] We mandate that each community proceed, in chapter, to analyze the context and the available resources before working out its community project. All the brothers shall endeavor to develop a sense of membership in the community in which they first build up God's Church, then are called to make [it] grow in the world through their preaching (cf. LCO 3 §II). The community shall gather regularly in Chapter under the capable leadership of the prior (cf. LCO 3 §II), whose responsibility it is to "promote regular fraternal and apostolic life," (cf. LCO 299, 1); the prior will thus play a determining role in the success of the community project.

210. [Recommendation] The community project should foster the harmony of Dominican life, integrating mission, quality of prayer life, time consecrated to personal study, as well as other aspects of regular observance (cf. LCO 1, IV).

Violence and community conflicts

211. [Congratulations] The Chapter expresses its concern, its close connection, and its gratitude for all the members of the Dominican family who live and witness within contexts plagued by violence, danger, and persecution.

212. [Exhortation] Since the witness of common life is the first way in which we preach against violence in the world, we encourage communities to schedule regular chapters of reconciliation into their yearly agendas (ACG Trogir 2013 66) in order to find ways to resolve destructive conflicts within our communities. Indeed, violence in our communities is never acceptable.

Canonical visitations as an instrument of government

213. [Declaration] If it is to be fruitful, the canonical visitation must take place within a climate of mutual listening and of dialogue, one which takes into account both the life context of each brother and the requirements specific to our democratic way of life.

214. [Recommendation] Taking into account the Acts of the General Chapters, specifically number 457 of Providence and 222-225 of Rome, canonical visitators, in addition to their individual meetings with the brethren, should at least discuss with the house chapter the ideas eventually to be included in the letter of evaluation; of course, the final decision remains up to the visitators alone. On those occasions when the Master of the Order himself comes for a visitation, this discussion will be carried out with the provincial council.

215. [Commission] On the occasion of his first canonical visitation of his term to the communities, the prior provincial shall discuss with the brothers gathered in Chapter the means by which the community project shall be set up, and he shall evaluate its effectiveness during his second canonical visitation (cf. LCO 311).

216. [Recommendation] We recommend that each province, in order to improve the provincials' visitations, should include in its statutes a pattern to be followed during these visitations.

217. [Ordination] Yearly meetings of provincial or regional priors, called by the prior provincial, should be instituted in order to foster exchanges and to facilitate the implementation of Provincial and General Chapters. This yearly meeting should be inserted into the statutes of the province.

The need for training in different forms of dialogue.

218. [Exhortation] We invite brothers to reflect on the articles concerning dialogue in the Acts of General Chapters beginning with that of Avila (1986) and those in the LCO.

219. [Exhortation] We exhort provinces, especially in formation, to prepare guidelines for promoting dialogue in all its aspects: fraternal dialogue, intercultural and interreligious dialogue, dialogue with people outside the Church, with the world of contemporary science and economics, between theology and pastoral work.

220. [Recommendation] We recommend that the Socius for the Intellectual Life, in collaboration with the Socius for the Apostolic Life and the Promoter for Justice and Peace, promote the planning of sessions and encounters dealing with ecumenical and interreligious dialogue. These initiatives shall be aimed particularly at brothers in formation so that they might relate intellectual consideration and concrete experience, and so to prepare themselves to confront the fundamentalist tendencies prevalent in today's world. (ACG Bogotá 2007 83, 102 ; ACG Rome 2010 162, 165 ; ACG Trogir 2013 96, 111).

The Balance between Convents and Houses

221. [Commendation] With regard to n. 167, on considering the proportion between convents and houses, we offer the following points for consideration, in addition to the LCO, to help in the identification of the advantages and disadvantages of having convents or houses, to discern the best proportion between them, to allow for an analysis, and to enable good decision-making for the future:

1) Convents enable regular life, but big convents can reduce the creativity of brothers and incline them to passivity in apostolic work. Envy and a tendency to settle for mediocrity can discourage the more active and creative brothers.
2) Houses reduce the democratic quality of our government, since, for example, superiors cannot be elected.
3) The number of brothers in a community is not as important as the quality of fraternal and apostolic life.

4) What are the economic circumstances of the foundation? Is it possible to sustain a big community financially in a given social environment?

5) Are there enough pastoral or apostolic demands for a big community? Have we a parish? What kind of apostolic challenges are there?

6) What size of community best supports fraternal cooperation and eliminates individualism?

7) The personal qualities and the level of human maturity of specific brothers are to be considered when founding communities.

8) The convents and houses of a province are the structures of its life and mission. Both convents and houses should nourish the Dominican charism effectively and maturely and not reduce it to the lowest common denominator.

9) In special cases, dispensation from the Curia can be asked (e.g. the size of a formation community).

With regard to aging brothers

222. [Declaration] Each community should show concern for its aging brothers. The commitment of these latter to serving the Church and the Order gives a human face to our history (cf. ACG Bogotá 2007, 173-175).

223. [Recommendation] We ask all the entities of the Order to do everything possible to enable aging friars to remain in their accustomed residences, and to offer them activities compatible with their capacities. Every entity must, within its given context, provide for one or several houses equipped to treat elderly brothers, as well as professional assistance should this be necessary.

224. [Exhortation] To this end, steps may be take in conjunction with other congregations or other types of institutions, providing places in specialized institutions where care can be offered to brothers who no longer can take care of themselves.

225. [Ordination] It is imperative that each entity provide the financial wherewithal, both medium and long term, to deal with aging.

226. [Recommendation] The lengthening of life and of its final stages raises numerous questions which sometimes call for delicate answers. For this reason, it is important for entities confronted with these problems to specify in their statutes the means by which competent authorities will be able to make necessary decisions. These means must take into account: due respect for the desire expressed by the friars, preferably in writing; the medical resources in their given situation; the legal requirements of each country and the cultural practices of each entity.

227. [Exhortation] In case it should become necessary to transfer a friar to a medical facility without his consent, it is preferable that this be handled by the prior provincial rather than by the conventual prior, who should try to convince the friar in question that the decision is necessary.

228. [Recommendation] We recommend that the prior provincial be sure that the proportion of elderly friars in the communities, particularly in formation communities, is conducive to living the mission of the community. In certain cases, he will need to make difficult decisions concerning assignments, acting always on behalf of the well-being of the mission and of the community.

229. [Recommendation] If, for reasons of mental health, a brother is unable to attend and thus to vote in a chapter, the prior shall discuss the matter with the conventual chapter, after which the major superior is informed and then ultimately makes the final decision (LCO 373.6).

Identity and Mission of Cooperator Brothers

230. [Recommendation] We ask the Coordinating Committee for Implementing the Dominican Cooperator Brothers Study to prepare, for the next General Chapter (2019), a text defining the identity and mission of the cooperator brothers within the Order so that the text can be integrated by that Chapter into the LCO as a special section.

Beatification of Brother Marie-Joseph Lagrange

231. [Commission] We charge the Master of the Order with the task of asking the Provinces to help the Province of Toulouse build up a

fund destined to support the cause for the beatification of Brother Marie-Joseph Lagrange.

Chapter VI: Vocation and Renewal

Promotion and care of one's vocation

232. [Declaration] By his very nature as a preacher, the Dominican friar is in continuous formation, in a constant process of integrating the essential elements of our preaching charism and challenges he has to face according to places and times. This process of formation likewise involves the assimilation of these values in each of the stages of a preacher's life, as a constant process of formation and renewal of our own vocation. (cf. ACG Rome 2010 200; ACG Trogir 2013 125)

233. [Exhortation] we exhort all friars to take responsibility for the promotion and care of their own vocation, to support and recognize as well their brothers and to promote favorable opportunities for communal reconciliation processes, so as to avoid isolation and a progressive loss of vocational fervor (cf. *Relatio* 2016, 58-60)

234. [Exhortation] We exhort all friars to create favorable opportunities for reconciliation. We joined the last general chapters (cf. ACG Trogir 2013 66; ACG Rome 2010 62.5) in calling all communities to face this reality and to hold regular reconciliation services for the brothers. The liturgical celebration of reconciliation should be included in the community project during the annual retreat.

Promotion and guidance of new vocations

235. [Declaration] We declare the urgent need to promote new vocations in the branches of the Order. All the brothers have to consider this promotion a priority, by which "we encouraged them to work with youth, especially the younger friars, and invite all the Dominican family to collaborate in promoting vocations, especially the nuns, with prayer, and encourage our communities to live visibly all the rich dimensions of Dominican life (ACG Rome 2010 188)." (cfr. RFG. 96)

Vocational Promotion

236. [Declaration] We declare that the promotion of vocations covers the cultivation of new vocations and the constant renewal and encouragement of the vocation of all the brothers as preachers of

the Gospel. We recognize that our loving response to God's call to be Dominicans involves a process of continuous renewal. Therefore, all the brothers are called to collaborate in promoting vocations both of new candidates as well as their own vocations. We invite young people to the Order because we want to share with them the Dominican vocation which we both want and value. The Dominican charism is an appealing call to them to the extent they perceive in us the joy of living faithfully all aspects of our life: prayer, common life of the brothers, study, and apostolic ministry. The friars renew their vocations by living the various dimensions of community life, and participating in retreats, renewal programs and special events during the Jubilee Year. Therefore, the promoter of vocations is to be understood as "promoter of new vocations." Since "every Dominican community is a school of preaching and a community in formation" (RFG, 57), the promoter of continuing formation and the leaders of our communities are the main promoters of our vocations.

237. [Exhortation] We urge and encourage all friars to pray for new vocations, while we work to promote them, as they are necessary so that the Order can continue fully to accomplish its mission in the Church.

238. [Exhortation] We exhort the major superiors to initiate collaborative vocation projects, to be courageous and with renewed energy to promote new vocations to Dominican life, recognizing that they are gifts of God for the Mission of the Order. (cf. ACG Trogir 2013 148).

239. [Exhortation] We exhort the friars to seek the renewal of their vocation and to promote a "culture of hospitality" in receiving candidates to share our community life, participating in various community activities, e.g. liturgical life, meals, recreation, etc. (RFG, 79). We urge the brothers to also promote vocations to the contemplative sisters.

Promotion of new vocations

240. [Ordination] We ordain the Provinces of the Order to appoint a Provincial Promoter of vocations with the primary role of

promotion of new vocations and coordinating of vocation ministry in his province. (Cf. RFG 97s .; ACG Trogir 2013 147)

241. [Exhortation] We urge the promoters of new vocations to diligently perform the following basic tasks in vocation ministry (Cf. RFG, 99):

1) To prepare materials for vocational promotion in parish bulletins, newsletters, brochures, postcards of saints of the Order and prayers, books, the use of mass media and the internet, among others;

2) To work with young people: vocational Retreats, youth ministry groups, chaplaincy in schools-university, attending vocation seminar meetings;

3) To encourage friars to help create a good receptive environment;

4) To help young people to discern their vocation and in case they want to join the Order, accompany them spiritually until they are accepted into the Order (RFG 100,105);

5) To collaborate with other entities and the Dominican Family.

242. [Exhortation] We urge superiors, to appoint a local vocation promoter, whose ministry will assist the Provincial Promoter to promote and coordinate local vocation promotion activities.

Formation processes

243. [Thanksgiving] We thank the Master of the Order, for having embraced the request of the General Chapter of Trogir (ACG Trogir 2013 132). He has drafted the new RFG.

244. [Ordination] We approve the official text [of the RFG] presented to the General Chapter and ask the Master of the Order for its distribution.

245. [Commission] We instruct the Priors Provincial and Vice Provincials to review the RFP and update the criteria for organization, development and evaluation of the processes of initial formation, using the revised criteria contained in the new RFG and taking into account the following elements:

1) Care that formation communities be truly representative of the apostolic and contemplative life of the Order.

2) Adjust the criteria for promotion, accompaniment and discernment of new vocations, supported on the main core and objectives of the plan of life and mission of the province.

3) During the time of initial formation provide an opportunity to better understand the reality of the province.

4) Encourage during initial formation, an experience outside their province, to confront, discover and encounter another culture, language, and church life, and other ways of being a friar preacher.

5) Planning for additional studies.

6) The role of the formation council, at the local and provincial level, in coordinating, evaluating and consolidating continuity between the different stages of formation.

7) The relationship between the formation council and prospective applicants and promotion of the apostolic plan of every province, continuously promoting the perspective that "forming preachers" be contextualized.

8) The formation of formators, accompanying them throughout the exercise of their office and arranging meetings with formators from other provinces.

9) Formation plan of cooperator brothers, adapted and integrated into the initial formation of all the friars.

10) A plan of study in accord with the personal qualities and needs of the Order for cooperator brothers. (Cf. ACG Trogir 2013 150ss)

Initial formation

246. [Exhortation] We urge the major superiors to form communities of solid formation, composed of mature and capable formators, in which the daily experience of an authentic Dominican life in respect and harmony, sharing with the capacity to overcome personal conflicts, so we can help the candidates to mature in their vocation (cf. ACG Trogir 2013 146)

247. [Exhortation] We ask the major superiors, the Socius for Formation and the Socius for the Intellectual Life to ensure good training for young people and to consolidate the mission of the Order:

1) To establish agreements of solidarity and help with other provinces that have difficulties in guaranteeing the initial formation, further studies and training of formators;

2) Organize exchanges between provinces, so that the new friars have the opportunity to discover, in their early years, other realities of the Order, other Dominican ecclesial apostolic and intellectual cultures.

248. [Admonition] We remind the major superiors, teachers and those masters in charge to dedicate themselves primarily to accompanying the brothers in order to guide and discern their vocation, frequently inviting experienced brothers and experts in religious life

Permanent formation

249. [Declaration] We declare that lifelong learning is not only to acquire pastoral and theological knowledge but also formation regarding human development of the friars, especially during the aging process to better integrate knowledge and skills, thus helping to promote fraternal ties and the preaching the Gospel. (cf. ACG Trogir 2013, 125; RFG 173s, 190-196).

250. [Exhortation] We exhort the major superiors to promote the professional training of brothers in various professional fields such as librarians, archivists, economics, management, fundraising, accounting, finance ... to help the institutions of the Order.

251. [Recommendation] We recommend that major superiors or regents of studies visit at least once a year the brothers who are assigned to another entity for reason of studies, to evaluate the progress of their studies, integration and participation in the life of the local community.

252. [Exhortation] We urge superiors to facilitate the friars' sabbaticals for rest, retreats, pilgrimages, studies, etc. at centers of the Order, or other centers, so they can renew their own vocation.

253. [Commendation] We recommend to superiors, in collaboration with the promoter of lifelong learning, to organize enrichment pro-grams for the older friars, including studies in humanities,

religious, apostolic and spiritual matters, to encourage a better life and mutual knowledge for all the brothers, old and young.

254. [Exhortation] We urge each brother to prepare for old age with a proper lifestyle, forming himself spiritually and culturally in order to better live this stage of his life. We also urge communities to plan and to include in the permanent formation program reflections on the "Art of Aging": how it affects the individual and community life.

255. [Ordination] We recognize the responsibility we have as ministers of the church to do everything possible to treat people under our pastoral care with the utmost dignity and respect. We apologize for the sins of the past in child abuse. We order all friars, especially those who are responsible for vocations and training, in discerning vocations to try to do everything possible to protect all people, especially children and youth, from inappropriate and harmful behaviors. (Cf. RFG, 18; ACG Bologna 1998 90; ACG Providence 2001 348-349; ACG Trogir 2013 142).

Collaboration with the Dominican Family

256. [Exhortation] We exhort the major superiors and those responsible for the Dominican Family to continue supporting each other and in a special way to move in the following areas of collaboration:

1) To create a *Commission of Formators* of the branches of the Dominican Family composed of teachers and masters in charge of the various stages of formation. The goal is to work on common formation programs and mutual support;

2) To establish a *Joint Vocation Promotion Team* for the promotion and cultivation of new vocations to all branches of the Dominican family;

3) Whenever possible, *to have continuing education together*, through meetings, retreats, training courses, celebrations, etc.;

4) To promote a community of lay Dominicans, Rosary Confraternity and the DJM (Dominican Youth Movement) in the entities of the Order as far as possible, accompanied by Dominican friars or sisters. And if they already exist to help in their formation and promotion among the faithful.

257. [Commendation] We recommend that the Master of the Order, assisted by the General Promoter of the nuns, show concern for the presence of our contemplative sisters in the historic monasteries of the Order in Spain (Caleruega, Segovia and Sto. Domingo el Real (Madrid)) so that they may continue to shine with a spiritual and community life. (Cf. ACG Providence 2001 325)

258. [Commission] We instruct the Master of the Order, with the help of the General Promoter of the nuns, to promote a meeting with the friars assisting the various Federations of Dominican contemplative nuns, to better accompany the nuns and meet the challenges presented by the latest standards issued by the Holy See.

Expressions of gratitude

259. [Thanksgiving] The General Chapter thanks all formators for the good work they do in the mission entrusted to them in the formation of friars preachers.

260. [Thanksgiving] We thank all brothers who work with generosity and creativity to ensure a good relationship between the different generations, and the care and attention given to older brothers and the sick.

261. [Thanksgiving] Recognizing the richness of the apostolic and evangelical witness of the different branches of the Dominican Family in the work of the Holy Preaching, we are grateful for the fraternity, shared witness and apostolate.

262. [Congratulation] We congratulate the brothers who organize and participate in training programs at the regional level, like the "Student Encounter (*Encuentro de estudiantes*) (CIDALC)," "Common Study Program," "Formator's courses," and "Leadership Conference" in the Asia Pacific region. Such collaborative programs help instill in our brothers the spirit of collaboration, and so we encourage them to continue.

263. [Congratulation] We congratulate the General Coordinator of the Jubilee of the Order and those who have collaborated in the pilgrimage, "In the Footsteps of St. Dominic," for student friars of

the Order (cf. ACG Trogir 2013 61.8) that enabled them to relive the apostolic experience of Saint Dominic. We also thank the sisters who joined in this fraternal Dominican journey.

Chapter VII: Constitutions and Ordinations

Preliminary Notes

To present a clearer picture of changes in LCO made by the Chapter, the same procedure is used as was employed in the Acts of previous General chapters.[1]

The numerical order of the LCO is followed. At each number specific signs show whether the text was approved for the first second or third time.

***   a confirmed constitution (three chapters)

**   an approved constitution (two chapters)

*   an introduced constitution (one chapter)
       (Note: If the approval or introduction of a constitution was made with an ordination, it is indicated by the sign [O].)

♦♦♦   Ordination definitively inserted in the LCO

♦♦   Ordination voted on for the second time, abrogating a previous ordination

♦   Ordination accepted for the first time

[A]   text that is abrogated

New texts are printed in *italics*.

Since a good interpretation of changes made demands a knowledge of the preceding text and its history, reference to the preceding chapter is made with the following signs:

   B = Bologna, 1998
   P = Providence, 2001
   K = Kraków, 2004
   Bo = Bogotá, 2007
   R = Rome, 2010
   T = Trogir, 2013

---

[1] Cf. ACG of Rome [1986], n. 307; Dublin, n. 188; Oakland, n. 208; Mexico, n. 248; Caleruega, ch. IX, p. 90; Bologna, n. 240; Providence, ch. X, p. 149; Kraków, n. 352, Bogotá, n. 288, Rome [2010], n. 262, and finally Trogir [2013].

This chapter sometimes changes texts "technically," although the substance of the law is not changed. The abbreviation "Techn." will mark such changes made whether to accommodate our laws to the CIC, or to harmonize the texts with other numbers of the LCO, or for a simple change in the rendering.

In our legislation what is said about convents applies also to houses unless expressly stipulated otherwise (LCO 260 §II).

In our legislation according to the purpose of LCO 252-256, by the name "province" is included proportionally vice provinces.

Constitutions

264. LCO 38 (P 472; K 353)

♦♦♦ 38. Ord. - § I. The brothers may have books and equipment for personal use *as determined by the provincial chapter.*
§ II. – When brothers have been assigned to another convent, they can take with them only *what has been determined by the provincial chapter and the provincial statute.*

265. LCO 43 (P 473; K 354)

♦♦♦ 43. Ord. - For a long journey or a prolonged absence a brother *needs the permission of the competent superior as determined by the provincial statute.*

266. LCO 97 (B 245; P 476; K 356)

♦♦♦ 97. Ord. I. For anyone to be promoted to the masterate in sacred theology, it is required:
1° – 2° (as in the text)
3° *be presented to the provincial chapter by the commission for the intellectual life of the province, and be approved by two thirds of the voters at the same chapter, or by the chapter of the province of affiliation or by the Master of the Order, if the brother is living in a convent or institute immediately subject to him;*

4° *a commission of at least three experts in the field of scientific specialization, chosen by the Master of the Order, pronounce favorably on the value of his work and his capacity to pursue it;*
5° - 6°.

267. LCO 139 (R 266; T 216)

♦♦♦ 139. Ord. – The brethren shall keep ever in mind the fact that their public statements (in books, newspapers, radio, and television, *and other instruments of social communication*) reflect not only on themselves but on their brothers, the Order, and the Church. For this reason, in reaching a judgement, they should be careful to foster a spirit of dialogue and mutual responsibility with their brothers and superiors. If their speaking or writing is about controversial issues, they should give special attention to this crucial dialogue with major superiors.

268. LCO 168

[Techn.] 168. Ord. - § II. - To admit into the Order those who have left it, or ~~another religious order~~ *another religious institute*, the prior consent of the provincial council is required, in addition to the following:

269. LCO 246

[Techn.] 246. Const. - [...] 4° are approved by the conventual council, whose duty it is to examine whether they have what is required for ordination; *(cf. CIC 1029 and 1051).*

270. LCO 253 §I

* 253. Const. § I. – A province consists of at least three convents, two of which must contain at least ~~ten~~ *eight* voters. Furthermore, each province must have at least forty voters.

271. LCO 256-bis (T 220)

♦♦ 256-bis. Ord. – § I. For the union *or fusion* ~~two~~ *of several* ~~entities (provinces, vice provinces or vicariates)~~ *provinces or vice provinces* the following are required:
1° ~~The vote of the council of each entity~~ *the consultative vote of the provincial councils* with respect to the ~~mutual~~ negotiations to be worked out about the union; *or fusion;*
2° *as circumstances dictate* consultation of the brethren and the chapters of all the convents and houses in the same entities, to be conducted in a way worked out in the individual entities;
~~3°- a special statute, approved by the Master of the Order, providing for a meeting for the chapter of each entity, enabling the entities to vote whether the union is to be proposed to the Master of~~

~~the Order; and providing also for the first assembly ad instar capituli of the new entity;~~

4° 3° the decision of the Master of the Order with his council; the first superior of the new *province or vice province* ~~entity~~ is appointed by the Master of the Order.

§ II ~~The union of two entities and the union or fusion of several entities should be done in the way described in § I, making the appropriate changes;~~ *If it seems necessary, a special statute of provisions may be promulgated by the Master of the Order.*

§ III If a province is to be divided, the procedures to be followed shall be worked out by the provincial council and approved by the Master of the Order with his council. ~~(B, n. 254)~~

(NB: An Ordination voted a second time with our various technical changes; we minimally confirm the deletion of the words "the decision of the Master of the Order... is appointed.")

272. LCO 257 §II (R 268; T 221)

*** [A] 257. Const. ~~§ II. In a territory where there is no province or vice province, and where there are local needs or a well-founded hope of making a permanent foundation of the Order, the Master of the Order may, with the consent of his council, erect a general vicariate with specific territory. He must first have consulted the brothers due to be assigned to the vicariate and the council of the relevant province. The statues by which the general vicariate is governed shall be prepared by the vicariate and approved by the Master of the Order and his council. In this case, after the brothers of the vicariate have been consulted, a vicar general is appointed, in the first instance, by the Master of the Order for four years. Relations between this general vicariate and other vicariates which may exist in the same place shall be determined according to n. 395.~~

273. LCO 258 (R 269; T 222)

** [A] 258. Const. § I. ~~If, for a period of three years, a province does not have three convents or thirty-five voters assigned in that province and habitually living there, the Master of the Order, having consulted his council, shall declare that it no longer enjoys the right to take part in general chapters as a province and shall reduce it to a vice province or general vicariate in accordance with n. 257, unless a general chapter has already been convoked.~~

§ II. ~~When a province which had been reduced to a vice province as provided for in § I, shall once again, for a period of three years, have~~

the necessary conditions, the Master of the Order must declare that it enjoys all its rights as a province.

** [O] 258. Const. – § I – *If some province or vice province does not meet the required conditions in n. 253 or n. 257 § I for three years, the general chapter or Master of the Order, with the consent of his council may declare that it no longer enjoys the rights of a province or vice province, saving always its right to participate in a general chapter already convoked;*
§ II. This declaration having been published, if the province meets the required conditions in n. 257. § I, it may enjoy the rights and bear the obligations of a vice province. Otherwise the Master of the Order may appoint a vicar (cfr. n. 400) in and over this province or vice province for four years, who would meet all the conditions required for a prior provincial, and he rules this entity according to the norms established by the Master of the Order.
§ III. If afterwards the province or vice province about which in § I fulfills the required conditions in 257 § I, the general chapter or Master of the Order with the consent of his council may declare it a vice province to enjoy the rights and bear the obligations.
§ III. *§ IV. –* In regions…

274. LCO 271 (B 257; P 486; K 363)

♦♦♦ 271. Ord. - §§ I - II. - (as in the text)
§III - A provincial chapter or prior provincial may assign a brother of another province to theirs, with the consent of the provincial chapter or of the prior provincial of the province of affiliation, the Master of the Order, having been informed.
§ IV. - A brother who in accordance with § I or § III has been assigned to a province also needs to be assigned to a specific convent.
§ V. - Direct or indirect assignations by reason of study must be made in writing (cf. Appendix n. 13).

275. LCO 285 (R 270 ; T 224)

♦♦♦ 285 Ord. – § I. –Ordinations which have remained in force through ~~five~~ *two* successive chapters and in the ~~sixth~~ *third* have been approved, shall be inserted in the book of constitutions and ordinations. *If they have not been inserted, they are to be considered abrogated, unless they are instituted again by a general chapter.*

276. **LCO 297-bis**

[Techn.] 297-bis. Const. In transacting business, that factor has the force of law which, the majority of those who must be convoked being present, is satisfactory to the majority absolutely, that is, which exceeds half the number of votes cast without counting invalid votes and abstentions *(cf. Appendix 14-bis)*.

277. **LCO 305 §II (P 487; K 364)**

♦♦♦ 305. Ord. - § II. – *If he is unable or unwilling to indicate his willingness to resign, the subprior, having heard the views of the council, must submit the case to the prior provincial.*

278. **LCO 309 §I (P 488; K 365)**

♦♦♦ 309. Ord. - § I. The chapter shall have a secretary, whom it elects in a single ballot. *He shall enter an account of discussions and resolutions in a book set aside for that purpose.*

279. **LCO 313**

[Techn.] 313. Ord. - §II - If the votes are tied, the chairman can postpone the decision for a short time before he settles the matter. ~~without prejudice to CCL 127, § I.~~

280. **LCO 318**

[Techn.] 318. Const. -It is the business of the council:
1°- 3° (as in the text);
4° to grant to those about to sit for an examination concerning their behavior ~~or to receive orders~~ the approval required by our legislation; *(cf. n. 245 et 251 § III)*;
5° to give approval for the reception of orders (cf. n. 246; CIC 1029 et 1051 §1);
~~5°~~ 6° to approve the report ... (as in the text)
~~6°~~ 7° to decide ... (as in the text).

281. **LCO 319**

[Techn.] 319. Ord. The council shall meet at least once a month and shall conduct its business according to the rules laid down above for the conventual chapter, nn. 312 and 313. *(cf. Appendix 14-bis)*.

282. **LCO 328 (R 272; T 226)**

♦♦♦ 328. Ord. – § I. – Any brother with active voting rights may be appointed bursar of the convent provided he is truly qualified for this office.

§ II. – He is appointed by the prior with the consent of his house council and the approval of the prior provincial.

§ ~~II.~~ III. – He is appointed for a three-year period and can be appointed immediately for another three years but not for a third time except ~~with the consent of the prior provincial~~ in case of necessity.

283. LCO 332 (R 273; T 227)

*** [A] 332. Const. - § I. – After the brothers in the house have been consulted, the superior of a house is appointed for three years by the prior provincial, ~~or by the regional prior, if the appointment concerns a brother assigned in a regional vicariate and unless the statutes of the vicariate provide otherwise~~. He may be appointed in the same manner for a further three years, but not for a third term.

§ II. At the end of the three-year period, the prior provincial ~~or regional prior~~ is obliged to appoint a superior within a month. However, a superior of a house shall remain in office until his successor is present in the house, unless the prior provincial determines otherwise.

284. LCO 341 (Bo 299)

♦♦♦ 341. Ord. – The prior provincial

1° at the end of a visitation, shall convey to the brothers his observations and ordinations in writing;

2° during the three months before leaving office, shall send a report on the state of the province to the Master of the Order, ensuring that it reaches him before the new election. *In this he shall report both on the brothers, whether "they are persevering in peace, assiduous in study, fervent in preaching and faithful in regular observance,"* [2] *and on the relationships between the province and convents and the ecclesiastical authorities.*

285. LCO 348 §I (Bo 300; R 274)

♦♦♦ 348. Ord. - § I – When a prior provincial ceases to hold office in accordance with n. 344, § I, the vicar of the province, as laid down in the statute of the province, will be: either the prior of the convent where

---

[2] Const. ed 1954, n. 452 § II.

the next provincial chapter is to be held or, if that convent does not have a prior at that time, the prior of the convent where the last chapter was held and so on, retrospectively; *or the prior who is senior by profession in the province*; or the prior provincial himself who has left office.

286. **LCO 352 §I (B 263; P 492)**

♦ 352. Ord. — The voters of a provincial chapter are:

§ I. – 1° regional priors;

2° *1°* vicars provincial elected according to the norm of n.389; *to the extent that they have voice according to n. 384-bis and the statutes of the vicariate*;

3° *2°* conventual priors; if the prior cannot attend on account of sickness or another grave reason accepted by the prior provincial, the subprior may take his place;

4° *3°* socii of priors going to a chapter, in accordance with n.490;

5° *4°* delegates of the brothers, in accord with nn. 497-501;

6° *5° a delegate of a non prioral house with at least four brothers with active voice in the territory of any nation where there is no other house of the same province;* [♦♦♦B 263; P 492]

7° *6° a pr*ior provincial who immediately before the chapter completed his term of office in that province.

(NB the words "delegate…. of the same province" are definitively inserted; the other changes, voted for the first time.)

287. **LCO 372**

[Techn.] 372. Const. - §III. If at any time the votes are tied, the president should by his vote break the tie *(cf. Appendix 14-bis).*

288. **LCO 373**

[Techn.] 373. Ord. - Among other things, the following must be dealt with in the provincial council:

1° the appointment or removal of a regional prior *vicar provincial* and of a conventual prior;

2° (as in the text)

289. **LCO 375 §I**

[Techn.] 375. Ord. - § I. –Two years after a prior provincial has been confirmed in office, he must summon to the next provincial council, in addition to its members, regional priors, vicars provincial, and conventual priors, unless the provincial chapter has determined otherwise regarding ~~regional priors,~~ vicars provincial, and priors in remote regions.

290. LCO 378 §II (R 276; T 230)

*** 378. Const. - § II. –The brother who will have fulfilled this office may be proposed immediately for a second term, but not a third, *unless with the consent of the Master of the Order.*

291. Chapter XIV - Art VI
Art. VI -On ~~Regional~~ Provincial Vicariates

292. LCO 384 (R 277; T 231)

*** [A] 384. Const. ~~§ I. When a province has outside its own territory in some nation or region at least fifteen vocals and one convent properly so called, a provincial chapter can unite them into a regional vicariate so that the apostolic activity and regular life of the brethren can be better coordinated.~~
~~§ II. It pertains to a regional vicariate: 1° to have its own statutes approved by a provincial chapter; 2° to celebrate its own chapters according to the norm of the vicariate statutes; 3° to admit candidates to the novitiate and to first profession; 4° to admit to solemn profession and sacred orders unless there is another provision in the provincial statute.~~

293. LCO 384 (R 277; T 232)

** [O] 384. Const. § I. *When, outside its own territory, a province has in another nation or region at least two houses of which one is a convent properly called, and at least fifteen vocals, a provincial chapter may unite them into a regional vicariate so that the apostolic activity and regular life of the brothers there can be better coordinated.*

*** § II. – *A provincial vicariate is governed by a statute made by the provincial chapter and approved by the Master General.*

294. LCO 384-bis (T 233)

♦♦ *384-bis. Ord. – The statute of the vicariate should determine:*
1° about the celebration of the vicariate chapter;
2° about the office of the vicar provincial who presides over the

vicariate as the vicar of the prior provincial;
3° about the officials of the vicariate;
4° about the instruction and promotion of vocations;
5° about the right of participating ex officio in the council and the chapter of the province (cf. 352 § I, 1°), with active voice or not;
6° about the faculties which the prior provincial, having consulted his council, may grant to the vicar about the admission of a candidate to the novitiate and for simple profession, about the assignment of the brethren to a house and convent of the vicariate, about the confirmation of conventual priors and the appointment of superiors of houses.

295. LCO 385

♦ [A] 385. Ord. —A regional prior is in charge of the vicariate and has, in addition to the faculties granted by the provincial chapter, the right to:

1º assign brothers who are in the vicariate, the rights of the prior provincial being respected;

2 º confirm a conventual prior according to n.467 and appoint superiors of houses according to n.332, unless the vicariate statutes provide otherwise;

3 º participate ex officio in the provincial council, unless something different has been determined in the provincial statutes;

4 º. participate ex officio in a provincial chapter (cf. 352 § I, 1°).

II. 1º A regional prior is elected for four years by the vocals assigned in the region and is confirmed by the prior provincial with the consent of his council;

2 º when the time for which the regional prior was elected has been fulfilled or when he has ceased to hold office in any way whatsoever, his office shall be exercised by the prior older in the Order in the same vicariate until the confirmation of a successor;

3 º what has been determined for a conventual prior in n.302,I, holds for a regional prior, with appropriate modifications.

296. LCO 386 §I (P 495; K 373)

♦♦♦ 386. Ord. — § I. In every vicariate there shall be a council whose consent or advice the ~~regional prior~~ *vicar provincial* must seek on important transactions according to the norm of vicariate statutes. The acts of this council after being collected are to be sent to the prior provincial.

(NB the ordination has been definitively inserted in the LCO with the technical changes.)

297. **LCO 386 §III**

♦386. Ord. - § III. ~~When [Quando]~~ *Since [Cum]* the prior provincial *with the provincial council* according to the norms in LCO or determined in the Statutes of the province or vicariate needs to treat *with the provincial council* of matters which concern the vicariate, he must *also* ~~first~~ consult the vicariate council ~~before consulting the provincial council~~; in cases where he confirms, appoints, or removes ~~the regional prior~~ *the vicar provincial*, he consults *only* the provincial council (cf. n. 373, 1°).

298. **LCO 388**

♦[A] ~~388. Ord. — The officials of a regional vicariate shall be appointed according to the norm of the statutes.~~ **LCO 391 (P 496; K 375).**

♦♦♦ 391. Ord. The following can be used to foster collaboration among the provinces of one region or nation:
1° - 5° (as in the text)
6° *the agreement of two provincial chapters or prior provincials for making a direct assignment from one province to a convent of another province, mindful of nn. 270 § I and II, 497 § I and 600, the Master General having been notified (cf. Appendix 16).*

299. **LCO 395 §I**

[Techn.] 395. Ord. - § I. -Conferences of priors provincial ~~and regional priors~~ as well as vicars shall be established according to nations or regions so that fraternal collaboration is truly organized and has a permanent character. These conferences shall be assembled regularly according to norms drawn up by the participating members and approved by the Master of the Order.

300. **LCO 407 (R 279; T 237)**

407. Const. – The following are assembled and have voice in an elective chapter:
§ I. – In the election of a Master of the Order:
1° - 3° (as in the text)
*** [A] 4° vice-provincials ~~and vicars general, concerning which~~

in n. 257;II;

5° - 6° (as in the text)

*** 7° a delegate from a province having at least twenty-*five* and up to one hundred brothers assigned in vicariates or houses of the province outside the boundaries of the province, elected from among them and by them according to provincial statute; furthermore, from a province having one hundred and one to two hundred brothers assigned in vicariates, another shall be elected delegate and so on in succession.

8° (as in the text)

301. **LCO 408 (R 280; T 242)**

408. Const. – The following are assembled and have voice in a general chapter of diffinitors:

1° - 3° (as in the text)

*** [A] 4° delegates elected from each vice province and general vicariate;

302. **LCO 409 (R 281; T 244)**

409. Const. – The following are assembled and have voice in a general chapter of priors provincial:

1° - 3°(as in the text)

*** [A] 4° each vice provincial and vicar general;

303. **LCO 409-bis (R 282 ; T 247)**

*** 409-bis. Const. – Each province which has at least twenty-*five* brothers assigned in vicariates or houses of the province outside the boundaries of the province has the right to send one delegate [...]

304. **LCO 417 §II (K 378)**

◆◆◆ 417. Ord. - § II. –

1° - 7° (as in the text)

8° A session by only vocals is held if a third part of the chapter either previously asked for it, or approved it by a vote requested by someone.

9° within two days... (as in the text)

10° in the acts... (as in the text)

11° as in the text... (as in the text)

305. **LCO 424**

[Techn.] 424. Const. - § I. – Under the chairmanship of the Master or vicar of the Order, or of their vicar, the general council is composed of the assistants of the Master of the Order and of the procurator general, whose consent or advice is required according to our laws and common law. *(cf. Appendix 14-bis).*

306. **LCO 425 §II**

[O] 425. Const. § II. – The assistants general of the Master of the Order are to be not less than eight and not more than ten. ~~Two~~ *Three* of them are put in charge of matters concerned with the apostolate and the intellectual life *and the fraternal life and formation* in the Order respectively, to the others is entrusted the concern for the relationship of the provinces with the Order, and for other matters which may be committed to them by the Master of the Order (cf. n. 428).

307. **LCO 427-bis**

♦ *427-bis. Ord. 427. — To the assistant for fraternal life and formation in the Order these especially pertain:*
1° to help the Master of the Order in all things which pertain to fraternal life and religious formation of the brethren, whether initial or ongoing [permanentem].
2° to help all the provinces, that they might provide for the religious formation of the brethren and for the flourishing of fraternal life;
3° when possible, to gather together the masters of initial formation as well as the promoters of permanent formation of one or several regions.
4° to facilitate for the provinces the instruction and the formation of the formators as well as the augmentation and execution of the plans of the provincials pertaining to ongoing formation.

308. **LCO 429 §II**

* [O] 429. Const. – § II - II. The appointment of the assistants for the apostolate, ~~and~~ for the intellectual life *and for fraternal life and formation* is to be made after all of the priors provincial have been heard.

309. **LCO 434 (T 252)**

♦♦ 434. Ord. – The postulator general for causes of beatification and canonization:

1° discharges his office according to the norms established by the Holy See and the statute approved by the Master of the Order;

2° at least once each year he is to render a report in writing to the Master General on the economic status, in which is described the monies received, and the balance of expenses, credits and debts;

2°–3° gives reports to each general chapter on the state of each cause.

310. **LCO 438 (P 505; K 381)**

♦♦♦ 438. Ord. - It is the duty of the promoter general for nuns and sisters:

1° to assist the Master of the Order and the procurator general in matters concerning the nuns and sisters;

2° (as in the text)

311. **LCO 455-bis**

♦ 455-bis. Ord. § I. – *If our laws so provide, election through letters can take place according to the following norms:*

1° within the time determined by the president, each vocal shall write his vote on a ballot in accord with n. 452, 6°;

2° then, after the ballot is placed in an envelope; he shall write in his own hand his name and place of residence on the carefully sealed envelope. After that he shall enclose the first envelope in another envelope and send it to the president [praeses] with another inscription so that it may easily be recognized.

§ II. –When the time determined for the reception of the ballots has elapsed, the president [praeses] with the provincial council or with two counters approved by the council should make the count.

1° when all the envelopes have been opened before the council or counters, the names of the electors written on the enclosed envelopes are examined to see if each of them has the required conditions for active voice; if anyone does not, the ballot is considered null and void;

2° the number of vocals and envelopes is compared

3° the envelopes are opened and destroyed before the ballots are unfolded;

 4° the ballots are examined in accord with n. 452, 9°, 10°, 11°;

5° if the majority for election or required for postulation is obtained, then the decree of election is drawn up by the one presiding, and the authentic instrument of election is prepared. All the vocals are to be informed of the outcome of the election;

6° if, however the absolute majority is not obtained in the first ballot, the presider should determine the time for a new and final ballot, and notify all the vocals of all that has taken place;

7° a provincial chapter, however, can determine whether to proceed to a third or even a fourth ballot, if in the second or third an absolute majority has not yet been obtained.

312. **LCO 455-ter**

♦ *455-ter. Ord. - § I – If our laws provide for an election by letter (cf. n. 455-bis), it also permits an election through electronic instruments.*

§ II – It pertains to the prior provincial with the consent of his council to discern if the election should proceed by letters or through electronic instrument, and to choose the electronic instrument which is fitting and of good repute.

§ III – An election through electronic instruments proceeds according to the following norms:

1° the presider sends to all the vocals instructions for accessing the electronic instrument chosen;

2° within the time established by the presider, each vocal should submit his ballot according to the received instructions;

3° When the time determined for the balloting has expired, the presider certifies its ending in the presence of the Provincial Council or of the two counters approved by the Council;

4° it proceeds in accord with n. 455-bis, § II, 5°, 6° and 7°.

§ IV – For the validity of an election through electronic instruments it is necessary that:

1° no vocal be excluded from the election because of the instrument chosen;

2° no brother having passive voice be excluded from the election of vocals because of the instrument chosen;

3° it be made certain that only the vocals cast a ballot, and no vocals cast multiple ballots;

4° the ballots of the individual vocals remain secret.

§ V – It pertains to the Provincial Chapter to establish other norms for elections through electronic instruments.

313. **LCO 465 (R 284; T 255)**

*** [A] 465. Const. – The election of a conventual prior must be confirmed by the prior provincial ~~or by the regional prior if it concerns a brother assigned to a regional vicariate and elected for a convent in that vicariate, unless the statute of the vicariate provides otherwise~~ (cf. Appendix n. 20).

314. **Chapter XVIII**
[Techn.]Chapter XVIII - The Election of a ~~Regional Prior and~~ Vicar Provincial
[Techn.] Art. I ~~- The Election of a Regional Prior~~

315. **LCO 477**
♦ 477. Ord. § I.– *If the statute of the vicariate shall have determined that the vicar be designated by election,* the president [praeses] of the election is that brother who actually governs the vicariate in accord with the norm ~~of 385, II, 2, or, if he is out of office, the senior in the Order from the superiors of that region.~~ *of the statute of the vicariate or perhaps another friar appointed by the prior provincial.*
§ II. – After consulting the ~~regional~~ *vicariate* council, it is for him to determine the time of the election and to notify all the voters; he must do this within a month of knowing that the office is vacant.

316. **LCO 479**
♦ 479. Ord. - § I. – Without prejudice to n. 443, for a person to be elected validly as ~~regional prior~~ *vicar provincial*, it is required that:
1° he be thirty years old and ten years from first profession;
2° he has not been ~~regional prior~~ *vicar provincial* in the same ~~region~~ *vicariate* for the two ~~four-year terms~~ *commissions* immediately preceding.
§ II. – If any brother cannot be elected because of the lack of one or more of the conditions mentioned in § I, 1° and 2°, the brothers may postulate him to the prior provincial who can ~~dispense from the interstices~~ make provision ~~and make provision~~ according to n. 467.

317. **LCO 480**
♦ 480. Ord. - § I. – It is *for the statute of the provincial vicariate* ~~for the provincial council or the regional council~~ to determine whether the voters must come together specially to hold the election or may vote by mail.

§ II. – If the election is carried out in a special assembly:

1° the president [praeses] and the place of the election shall be as in n.477;

2° in the actual process of the election, n.464 shall be observed (cf. Appendix n. 18).

§ III. If, however, the vocals cannot gather together conveniently, the ~~following~~ norms in *n. 455-bis* shall be used:

1° ~~within the time determined by the president (n.477, § II), each vocal shall write his vote on a paper ballot in accord with n.452,6;~~

2° ~~then, after placing the paper ballot in an envelope, he shall write in his own hand his name and place of residence on the envelope and seal it carefully. After that, he shall enclose the first envelope in another envelope and send it to the president [praeses] with a special marking so that it can easily be recognized.~~

§ IV. – When the time determined for receiving the paper ballots has elapsed, the president [praeses] with the ~~regional council~~ *counters* shall conduct the count *in accord with n. 455-bis §II and according to the following norms:*

1° ~~when all the external envelopes have been opened in the presence of the council, the names of the electors written on the outside of the inner envelopes are examined to see whether each of them has the conditions required for active voice; if anyone does not, his vote shall be considered null and void;~~

2° ~~the number of vocals and of envelopes is compared;~~

3° ~~the envelopes are opened and burned before the ballots are unfolded;~~

4° ~~the votes are then examined in accordance with n.452, 10, 11, and 12;~~

~~5°~~ 1° if the majority required for election or postulation is obtained, a decree of election shall be drawn up by the president [praeses], and an authentic document of the election shall be prepared and sent to the prior provincial in accord with n. 453, I (cf. Appendix n. 24). All the voters shall be notified by letter of the result of the election;

6° ~~if, however, an absolute majority is not obtained in the first ballot, the president (praeses) with the council shall fix the time for holding a new and final ballot and shall inform by letter both the prior provincial and the voters of all that has taken place;~~

7° ~~a provincial chapter, however, can determine that a third or even a fourth ballot may be held if in the second or third an absolute majority is not obtained;~~

8.° 2° but in the final scrutiny, whether it is the second (n. 455-bis §II, 6°), or the third or the fourth (n. 455-bis §II, 7°), if an absolute majority is not obtained, provision of the office reverts to the prior provincial. (cf. n. 464).

318. **LCO 481 (R 285; T 257)**

*** [A] 481. Const. §I. For the confirmation or cassation of the election of a regional prior and his acceptance, nn. 465-473 shall be observed.

II. The right of appointing a regional prior reverts to the prior provincial, n.373,1, being observed:

1° when at the time of the vacancy in the office of regional prior, the vicariate does not have the conditions stated in n.384; then, however, nn. 483 and 484 must be observed in the appointment of a vicar;

2° when all the vocals shall have renounced their voice and shall not have been reinstated by the prior provincial;

3° when for any reason whatsoever a regional prior has not been elected or postulated within six months of the known vacancy;

4° when in the process of election there have been seven futile scrutinies (cf. n.480, II, 2);

5° when the brethren elect the same brother again after the first election has been cassated, unless that election was cassated only because of procedural form and not because of the character of the one elected;

6° when there have been two or at most three elections confirmed by the prior provincial and not accepted by those elected; then after the second election the prior provincial can, and, after the third he must, appoint a regional prior.

319. **LCO 481**

♦ 481. *Ord. § I. –Regarding the confirmation or cassation of the election of a vicar provincial and his acceptance, the norms in nn. 465-473 are to be observed.*

§ II. – The right of instituting a vicar provincial devolves to the prior provincial, respecting n. 373,1°:

1° when the vicariate, at the time of a vacancy of the provincial vicar, does not have the conditions referred to in n. 384 §I; then, however, in the institution of a vicar, the vocals of the convents of the vicariate should be heard according to the norm of the vicariate statutes;

2° when all the vocals have renounced their voices they should not be restored by the prior provincial;

3° when, for whatever reason whatsoever within six months from a known vacancy, the vicar provincial has not been elected or postulated;

4° when in the process of an election in a special gathering there have been seven unsuccessful ballots (cf. n. 480, §II, 2°);

5° when in the process of an election by letters there have resulted two unsuccessful ballots (cf. n. 480 §IV, 2°), or three or four if the provincial chapter has so determined (cf. n. 455-bis §II, 7°);

6° when the brethren, the first election having been cassated, elect the same brother again, unless the first election was cassated just because of procedure and not because of the person elected;

7° when two or at most three elections have been taken and confirmed by the prior provincial but not accepted by the one elected; then, indeed, after the second election the prior provincial may, and after the third ought to appoint a vicar provincial.

320. **Chapter XVIII - Art. II**

[Techn.] Art. II -- On the Election of a Vicar Provincial

321. **LCO 482 (R 286 ; T 258)**

*** [A] 482. What has been established in nn. 477-481 for the election of a regional prior applies also, with appropriate modifications, to the election of a vicar provincial (cf. n.389).

322. **LCO 483 (R 287 ; T 259)**

*** [A] 483. When a vicar provincial must be appointed by the prior provincial, the brethren, who in accord with n.478 would have active voice in the election, shall first be consulted (cf. Appendix n. 24).

323. **LCO 484**

♦ [A] 484. Ord. -§ I. The consultation of the vocals shall be made through letters to be sent to the prior provincial in which each vocal shall indicate three names according to his order of preference.

§ II. The prior provincial shall appoint as vicar provincial one of the three who received a greater number of votes unless he shall have judged.

324. **LCO 494 (P 507; K 382)**

♦♦♦ 494. Ord. - *§ I. – In convents where one socius is to be elected, the election is held according to the manner indicated in the norm of n. 452.*
§ II. - In convents where several socii are to be elected (cf. n.490, § II), it is to be determined by secret vote whether all together or one is elected after another.
§ III. - Before the election, by a majority consent of the vocals, the manner of electing should be decided.
§ IV. - An election is performed in the following manner:
1° if all the socii are elected together, the election is terminated in the seventh ballot in which a relative majority suffices;
2° if, however, one is elected after another, then for each socius, if up to the third ballot inclusively no candidate receives an absolute majority of the votes, in the fourth and final ballot only those two are to be presented who in the preceding ballot received the majority of the votes, still observing n. 450, § III.

325. **LCO 497 (T 260)**

** [A] 497. Const. – § I. – While observing n.491, § II, and with the exception of those who according to the norm of number 352, I, and § III are already represented the following elect a delegate to a provincial chapter, provided they enjoy active voice (cf. nn. 440 and 441):
1° (as in the text);
2° ~~unless it is indicated otherwise~~ in the statute of the province, brothers directly assigned to houses or convents under the immediate jurisdiction of the Master of the Order, excepting always those who belong to the general council;
3° - 4° (as in the text)

326. **LCO 499 §§I - II (T 262)**

♦♦ [A] 499. Ord. – § I. – It pertains to the provincial council or to the regional council to determine for each elective college whether the vocals must meet in special session to hold the election or vote by mail.
§ II. If the election is to be held in a special assembly:
1° the president [praeses] and place of the election shall be determined by the provincial ~~or regional council~~;
2° - 3° (as in the text)

327. **LCO 499 §III**

♦ 499. Ord. - § III. If, however, the vocals cannot gather together conveniently, ~~it takes place~~ *it proceeds by mail, the prior provincial presiding, in accord with n. 455-bis and* according to the following norms:

~~1°. each vocal shall write his vote on a ballot and send it in a double envelope to the prior provincial or regional prior in accord with n.480, III;~~

~~2°. when the time determined for the reception of ballots has elapsed, the prior provincial or the regional prior with his council shall make the scrutiny in accord with n.480, IV, 1°-4°;~~

~~3 ° if the majority required for election is obtained, all vocals shall be informed by letter of the result of the election;~~

~~4°~~ 1° if, ~~however~~, an absolute majority is not obtained in the first scrutiny, the prior provincial ~~or regional prior~~ with his council shall proceed according to the norms of n.~~480, IV, 6 °, and 7 °.~~ *455 bis, § II, 6° and 7°*. In the final scrutiny, whether it is the second (n. 6°), or third or fourth (n. 7°), only those two can be presented who achieved the greater number of votes, with n. 450, §III remaining in force;

~~5°~~ 2° in the event of the incapacity of a delegate, he shall be judged to be the substitute who in the final scrutiny obtained second place according to the number of votes, n.450, §III, being observed.

328. **LCO 560 §§I, III & IV (K 384)**

♦♦♦ 560. Ord. - *§ I. – Entities of the Order should define through Chapters or in statutes the way of handling monetary goods (management; care of money, transactions, liabilities or the like; depositing and management in banks) according to the special conditions of the place.*

§ II. - (as in the text)

§ III. – Monies shall be deposited only in banks the security of which is established beyond doubt, and, in accord with the purpose of n.555, they shall be deposited in the name of the respective moral person or institute to which they belong.

§ IV. – The bank shall be chosen by the administrator himself with the consent of the superior.

329. **LCO 563 §II**

[Techn.] 563. Ord. § II - Every year, the superior of a house, the conventual prior, and the vicar provincial, ~~and the regional prior~~ shall send to the prior provincial an accurate and complete report prepared by the syndic in which a budget for the following year is included, made after consultation with the conventual chapter if the provincial chapter shall have determined this and approved by the council of the convent or the vicariate; copies of this budget shall be kept in the files of each syndic.

330. **LCO 566 §I**

[Techn.] 566. Ord. - § I. Every year, the syndic of the province and vice province ~~and general vicariate~~ shall present to his respective council an accurate and complete report on the revenues and expenses, debits and credits of the same entity, on the transactions he has made, and on the economic condition of the entity; he shall also propose a budget or estimate for the following year. All these reports must be approved by the respective council. Furthermore, the syndic must submit his economic report to the superior of the entity each month.

331. **LCO 566 §II**

[Techn.] 566 Ord. - § The ~~regional prior and~~ vicar provincial likewise should submit to his prior provincial an accurate financial report approved by ~~respective councils~~ the council in the same way as instituted above in § I.

332. **LCO 567 (Bo 312; R 291)**

♦♦♦ 567. Ord. *Each year, before the end of the month of August, with the assistance of their syndics, priors provincials, vice-provincials, ~~vicar generals~~ and prefects of institutes under the immediate jurisdiction of the Master of the Order should send their economic reports directly to the Master of the Order:*
1° The annual economic report, i.e., a complete accounting of the economic status of their respective entities. In it they are to describe the monies received, expenses, interest received and paid, proposed annual budget, as well as the individual projects planned or begun. If, however, it has several vicariates, convents, houses or institutes, the same is to be done for each. Although the form of this report for other places can be different, the report should contain the whole testimony required here. To facilitate this, a sample of this form is to be available from the syndic of the Order.

2° A response regarding the contribution by taxation, necessary for annually computing the contributions of the entities of the Order. For from the response is derived the amount of assets to be allocated for the formation of the brethren, as well as for the care for the illnesses of the brethren, and in subsidizing other entities of the Order, and how much of the payment remains. To this end an annual questionnaire is sent by the syndic of the Order, the same form for all the entities.

(NB: The Ordination is definitively inserted in the LCO abrogating the words "vicar generals.")

333. **LCO 575 §II (P 513; K 387)**

♦♦♦ *575. Ord. - § II – Concerning the expenses of a general chapter, the following must be kept in mind:*
1° travel expenses are paid in the so called averaging manner so that each individual capitular in fact is paid the same sum of money;
2° expense grants and general expenses for the chapter shall be paid proportionately by the General Curia and by each province, among which equity and proportion ought to be observed, according to the manner established in the chapter itself.
3° six months before the convocation of a general chapter, the syndic of the Order and the syndic of the convent where the chapter is to be held shall prepare a budget or the projected expenses of the chapter to be submitted to the Master of the Order with his council. Afterwards, it shall be sent to each province for consultation.

334. **Appendix 11**

[A] Appendix 11 Declaration on the name "province," (252, 256). From the Acts of the general chapter of Caleruega, celebrated in 1995, n. 201: With respect to LCO nn. 252, 256 we declare that by the name of "province" is understood vice-provinces and general vicariates (nn. 257, 259) unless stipulated otherwise.

335. **Appendix 12**

Appendix 12 - List of provinces and vice provinces and general vicariates of the Order. (259, § I)

336. Appendix 13A - Letter of Direct Assignment

I, Brother N.N., Prior Provincial of the Province of N.,
to our beloved Brother N.N.

Considering the needs of the Province and your ability in the service of Christ, by virtue of this document *and by the authority of my office*, I revoke your former assignation from the convent (or house) in which at present you are assigned, and I assign you simply to the convent (or house) of N, and I direct *you in virtue of obedience that within so many days (or promptly; or as quickly as convenient) to travel to the said convent (or to the said house) and move yourself there. Moreover, I direct* the superior of the said convent (or house) to receive you kindly and treat you charitably, as legitimately assigned.

Given at N., in the Convent of N., under the seal of the Province, on the ... day of the month of ..., in the year of our Lord ...

(Seal of the Province)
Brother N.N., O.P.
Reg. pag. Prior Provincial
Brother N.N., O.P.

Ordinations

We renew the following ordinations of previous general chapters:

Official Languages

337. The official languages of the Order are English, Spanish and French because of their international character. These languages will be used in all documents of the Order and by the Master of the Order. They will be spoken in the General Chapters. For legal texts, Latin remains the language (B 200).

Formation in administration

338. We ordain that the moderator of studies organize for students during their institutional studies a seminar or course on practical management of monies (B 224).

LCO

339. We ordain that modifications to the LCO appear promptly on the Order's website (cf. K 241).

Syndic's report

340. We ordain that in the year in which we gather for General Chapter the *Relatio* of the Syndic of the Order be approved by the Master and his Council after being studied, analyzed and recommended by the Economic Council of the Order. The *Relatio* should be presented to the general assembly of the Chapter, together with the *Relatio* of the Master (R 243).

Friars who repeatedly refuse to hand over their income to the community

341. We ordain that all priors provincial and vicars provincial, with their respective councils, and in accordance with LCO 32 §II, establish and implement norms to be followed in regard to those friars who repeatedly refuse to hand over their income to the community in spite of fraternal correction (cf. K 238, T 75).

Brothers outside community

342. We ordain that all priors provincial and vicars provincial review every year the situation of brothers who have been outside community for long periods of time, taking into account the Constitutions of the Order and Canon Law (T 76).

Promoters of communications media

343. Bearing in mind that the internet is both a communications medium requiring technical expertise and a new area of communication requiring new methods and styles, we ordain the Provinces to name a promoter of media, charged with the task of promoting and coordinating initiatives in this field at the level of each province. Each promoter will inform the curia of his appointment in order to be included in the wider network, "Order of Preachers for Technology, Information, and Communication" (OPTIC), under the coordination of the General Promoter for Media. (T 115).

Statutes of Vicariates

344. In view of LCO 362 §IV and LCO 384 §II we ordain that the Master of the Order, when approving the Acts of a Provincial Chapter, shall ensure that the statute of a vicariate permits a necessary autonomy to the vicariate in view of its distinct cultural and geographical circumstances, while also making the strongest possible provision for the proper concern for and support of the mission in the vicariate by the Province (cf. T 168).

Appointment of Provincial Promoter for the Lay Fraternities or Religious Assistant

345. We ordain that, when a prior provincial wishes to nominate as Provincial Promoter for the Lay Fraternities or as Religious Assistant for one or more Fraternities, someone who is under a jurisdiction other than that of the brothers of the Order, this shall only take place with the prior written agreement of the competent authority. We also ask the Master of the Order to insert this condition into the norms of the Lay Fraternities (T 187).

Directories of the Dominican Laity

346. We ordain that the directories of the Dominican Laity, national or provincial, be approved by the provincial with his council in the province(s) in which these entities are established (T 188).

Permanent Commission for promotion of studies

347. We replace the ordinations of the General Chapter of Rome 2010 97-100, with the following:

We order that the standing committee for the promotion of studies in the Order ensure that the academic and research centers are developing strategic plans and that it evaluate the implementation of these plans. [R 97]

We order that the members of the Permanent Commission for the Promotion of Studies in the Order are:

1) the Socius of the Master of the Order for Intellectual Life, President of the Commission;
2) the coordinators of the regents of the different regions that make up the Order proposed by the regions and confirmed by the Master of the Order for a period of six years;
3) a representative of the academic institutions under the immediate jurisdiction of the Master of the Order, appointed by the Master of the Order;
4) two other members appointed by the Master of the Order which, if possible, at least one who is linked to our universities. [R 98, except n. 2]

We order that the members of the Permanent Commission for the Promotion of Studies in the Order appointed by the Master of the Order are appointed for six years [R 99].

We order that the Standing Committee for the Promotion of Studies in the Order assists the Master of the Order and the Socius for the Intellectual Life in the following areas:

1) planning and allocation of human and financial resources of the Order in the field of study;
2) promoting the training of future teachers;

3) the implementation of the new *Ratio Studiorum Generalis*;
4) preparation of a report on the viability of the study centers of the Order prior to each General Chapter;
5) supporting the development of the report the Socius for the Intellectual Life must present to the General Chapter, and the development of proposals to be presented to the Chapter;
6) checking the status of the publications that depend on the Master of the Order and the establishment of a policy for publication and dissemination.
7) other tasks that are required by the *Ratio Studiorum Generalis* [cf. R 100].

Safeguarding

348. We replace the ordination of the General Chapter of Rome 2010 236, with the following: We acknowledge that effective protection of children and other vulnerable people and a commitment to ensure their human and spiritual development, in keeping with the dignity of the human person, are integral parts of the Gospel message that we are called to preach (cf. Pope Francis, *Chirograph for the Establishment of the Pontifical Commission for the Protection of Minors*, 22 March 2014).

Seeking to be preachers of the reconciliation and healing found in Christ (LCO 2 §I), we ordain that:

1) Priors provincial are to ensure that the brothers are educated in the importance of promoting safe practice, minimizing risks of abuse and maximizing the response to reports of concern. This is to begin from the time of initial formation and be regularly renewed, in compliance with the programs offered in dioceses or by conferences of religious. Where there are no such programs, Provinces are to use the ones most suited to them as formulated by other Dominican entities.
2) Priors provincial and their councils must ensure that each province has clear and detailed policies and procedures that properly address questions of ensuring safe environments, pastoral care, and responding to concerns and allegations of abuse. These policies are to be in conformity with the norms of canon and civil law. Rights of complainants and brothers against

whom allegations are made are to be protected and maintained.

3) These policies and procedures are to be kept under review. When they are updated, copies are to be distributed to all the brothers of the Province, and one copy sent to the Master of the Order.

List of provinces and vice provinces of the Order

349. [Commission] We commission the General Curia to update Appendix 12 of LCO (list of provinces and vice provinces of the Order).

Changes to appendices of LCO necessary as a result of restructuring

350. [Commission] We commission the General Curia to make the textual changes to the appendices of LCO necessary as a result of restructuring of general, regional and provincial vicariates.

Vice provinces not fulfilling the requirements

351. [Declaration] We declare that, for the remaining general vicariates, the norms for vice provinces not fulfilling the requirements of LCO 257 §I shall be applied until a permanent solution is found for their status.

Assignations to convents within a vicariate

352. [Declaration] In accordance with LCO 270 §I we declare that assignation is the appointment of a brother to a province or to a specific convent. As a structure internal to a province, it is not possible to assign a brother to a provincial vicariate, only to a particular convent within the vicariate. *Per se*, the authority to assign a brother from outside the vicariate to a convent of the vicariate lies with the prior provincial.

Nevertheless, the prior provincial may choose to delegate to the vicar provincial the authority to assign a brother to a convent of the vicariate, leaving the choice of the particular convent to the prudent discretion of the vicar provincial. Such delegations are to be made in writing, naming the brother to be assigned. The following formula may be used:

Brother N.N., Prior Provincial of the Province of N., to our beloved brother N.N., Vicar Provincial of the Vicariate of N.:

Considering the needs of the Province and your Vicariate, and the usefulness in Christ of our brother N.N., I am inclined to make him available for service in the said Vicariate. Therefore, by virtue of this letter, I delegate to you the authority to revoke the assignation of the said brother N.N. to the convent (or house) in which he is currently assigned and to assign him simply to a convent or house of the Vicariate of N. according to your prudent discretion within three months from the date of this letter. I furthermore direct you to receive our brother kindly and treat him charitably once he is legitimately assigned.
Given at N., in the Convent of N., under the seal of the Province, on the ... day of the month of ..., in the year of our Lord ...

(Seal of the Province)
Brother N.N., O.P. Reg. Prior Provincial
Brother N.N., O.P. Secretary
Reg. pag.

The letter of assignation should mention the delegation from the prior provincial thus:
Brother N.N., Vicar Provincial of the Vicariate of N., delegated by brother N.N., Prior Provincial of the Province of N., to our beloved brother N.N.:
Considering the needs of the Province... (as in LCO, Appendix 13A)

These texts may be used with suitable adaptations also for assignations made in accordance with LCO 271 §III or LCO 391, 6° (cf. also LCO, Appendix 13B).

Rule of the Priestly Fraternities

353. [Commission] We commission the Master of the Order with the General Council to examine and respond appropriately to the proposals made by the International Meeting of the Priestly Fraternities of St. Dominic of February 2016, in collaboration with the Coordinator of the Priestly Fraternities. In accordance with the commission of the General Chapter of Rome 2010 233, we commission the Master of the Order to approach the Holy See to

make any amendments to the Rule of the Priestly Fraternities which may be necessary.

Ordinations of previous general chapters

354. [Declaration] Taking into account the modification introduced into LCO 285 with respect to ordinations of General Chapters (cf. R 270, T 224), and in order to avoid any ambiguity, we declare that the ordinations of previous general chapters which have neither been renewed nor inserted into the LCO at this Chapter are considered abrogated, either because they have been fulfilled or because they are no longer necessary.

Chapter VIII: Economic Commission

Financial Administration

355. [Declaration] The syndic of the Order, fr. Hilario Provecho Álvarez, OP, in accordance with LCO 569, has presented a report of his administration of the General Curia for the fiscal years 2013 – 2015. The report was approved by the Chapter.

356. [Declaration]The syndic of the Order, fr. Hilario Provecho Álvarez, OP, in accordance with LCO 569, has presented the accounts of the General Curia for the fiscal years 2013 – 2015. The accounts were approved by the Chapter.

357. [Declaration] We declare that the following accounts: the Solidarity Fund; the Saint Dominic Fund; the Dominic Renouard Fund; the Francisco de Vitoria Fund; the Master of the Order Fund; the Leonine Commission Fund; and the Administrative Funds for the Entities under the Immediate Jurisdiction of the Master of the Order have been studied by the Economic Council of the Order and approved by the Master of the Order and the General Council.

358. [Declaration] We declare that, in accordance with LCO 571, the financial reports of the convents and institutes under the immediate jurisdiction of the Master of the Order, promptly sent to the Master, were approved by their respective councils. These reports have been studied by the Economic Council of the Order and approved by the Master of the Order and the General Council.

359. [Thanksgiving] We thank the syndic of the Order, fr. Hilario Provecho Álvarez, OP, and the Economic Council for their contribution to the economic administration of the Order.

Regional Meetings

360. [Ordination] Given the fact that the need for regional meetings of the syndics of the entities in their region varies from one region to the other, we ordain that Act 199 of the General Chapter of Trogir (ACG 2013 Trogir 199) be abrogated and that the initiative for organizing such meetings be left to the regional socius.

Annual Contributions to the Order

361. [Declaration] We declare that the deductible formation expenses referred to in LCO 567 include formation expenses for the pre-novitiate, provided the approved RFP of the concerned entity includes a pre-novitiate program.

362. [Ordination] We ordain that the ordinary contribution of every province and vice- province to the General Curia be no less than €3,000 (ACG 2013 Trogir 206).

363. [Ordination] We ordain that the contribution of convents and other institutions under the immediate jurisdiction of the Master of the Order be 6% of their gross revenues (ACG 2013 Trogir 207).

364. [Ordination] In line with the General Chapters of Rome (ACG 2010 Rome 249) and Trogir (ACG 2013 Trogir 201), we ordain that the annual contribution of each province and vice-province to the budget of the General Curia shall be determined in accordance with the norms of the General Chapter of Bogotá (ACG 2007 Bogotá 261), including medical and health care costs as well as the costs of formation.

Contributions from the Order

365. [Ordination] We ordain that the Syndic of the Order include in the budget of the General Curia an annual subsidy to the following entities:
   1) University of St. Thomas (Angelicum): €150,000 intended for ordinary operating expenses.
   2) Convent of St. Dominic and St. Sixtus at the Angelicum: €40,000 (ACG 2007 Bogotá 276), which will cover the expenses of friars assigned simpliciter.
   3) École Biblique et Archéologique: €15,000 for supporting the research activities of the brothers teaching at the École Biblique.
   4) Inter-Africa (IAOP): €150,000 proportionately distributed according to the number of friars in each sub-region for the initial formation of the friars.
   5) Asia/Pacific: €50,000 for formation projects and regional projects.

6) Latin America and the Caribbean (CIDALC): €25,000 for regional projects.

366. [Ordination] We ordain that the amount of expenditures that the Master of the Order may authorize without needing the approval of his council shall not exceed €75,000 (ACG 2013 Trogir 202).

367. [Commission] Given the fact that the fund for the postulation office is depleted, given the complexity of the new rules regarding the financing of postulation from the Congregation for the Causes of Saints and given the need to promote the Saints and Blesseds of the Order, we commission the Master and his Council to set up a committee to assess the financial needs to achieve the objectives of postulation and to set up measures for the proper financial administration of the office.

368. [Commission] We commission the Master of the Order and his Council to modify the program of aid to provinces and vice-provinces of the friars who are serving at the Curia or in the institutions under the immediate jurisdiction of the Master of the Order, in order to ensure a retirement fund for the latter, in such a way as to include friars older than 65 years, as long as they serve at the Curia or in institutions under the immediate jurisdiction of the Master of the Order and do not receive any form of pension.

Costs of the Chapter

369. [Ordination] We ordain that the cost of the General Chapter should be shared equitably, reflecting the portion that each entity contributes annually to the regular budget of the Order. Transportation costs are to be divided equally among all and administrative costs proportionately. Each delegate must pay the actual per diem cost (ACG 2007 Bogotá 286; ACG 2010 Rome 260, ACG 2013 Trogir 208).

Solidarity

370. [Thanksgiving/exhortation] We thank those entities which offer concrete support to entities in the Order with less financial resources for the realization of their projects and for the formation of their brothers. We exhort all entities of the Order to explore further ways in which this work of solidarity can be promoted.

Projects that make the entity more self-reliant should be encouraged.

371. [Exhortation] We exhort the brothers of the Order to explore and promote the ways in which they can express solidarity with brothers in areas of extreme suffering and conflict.

372. In order to move from a culture of charity to a culture of solidarity in the Order and given the fact that more financial resources are required in the short and long term to achieve this objective, *Spem Miram Internationalis* should be strengthened. Therefore:

373. [Ordination]We ordain, during this Jubilee period, an increase of 10% of the annual contribution of each entity, which should go directly to and be divided equally among the two endowment funds of *Spem Miram Internationalis* until the next General Chapter.

374. [Commission]We commission *Spem Miram Internationalis* to make known to all entities of the Order its existence and the projects it supports.

375. [Commission] We commission *Spem Miram Internationalis* to develop new ways to increase its capital, e.g., inviting entities to make loans for specific periods, to be invested by *Spem Miram*, which would use the interest generated thereby.

376. [Exhortation] We exhort all entities to notify *Spem Miram Internationalis* when a sizeable act of solidarity is made to any project so that any further funding of the project by *Spem Miram* can be properly assessed.

377. [Commission] We commission *Spem Miram Internationalis* to investigate the possibility of appointing an assistant to its president for its management and promotion.

378. [Ordination] We ordain that the president of *Spem Miram Internationalis* submit an annual report to the priors provincial and vice-provincials (ACG 2013 Trogir 203) and present the financial accounts to the General Chapter for its approval.

379. [Congratulation] We thank fr. Dominic Izzo, OP, and the Governing Board of *Spem Miram Internationalis* for its development and for promoting solidarity in the Order.

Thanksgivings

380. [Thanksgiving] The General Chapter of Bologna expresses its warmest gratitude to all who contributed to the preparation and successful outcome of the Chapter, namely:
    - the Province of San Domenico in Italia, which hosted the chapter, and the community of the Patriarchal Convent of San Domenico;
    - the brothers and sisters who worked so hard as members of the secretariat, all those assigned to simultaneous translation and translation of texts, those who prepared liturgies, those who wrote the minutes, and all others who according to their particular functions greatly assisted the Chapter;
    - the staff of Ospitalità San Tommaso who took such good care of us.

Site of the Next General Chapter

381. [Declaration] We declare that the next General Chapter, which will be an elective chapter, will be celebrated in the convent of Ho Chi Minh City (Saigon) Vietnam, in July – August 2019, the exact date to be fixed later.

Suffrages for the Living

For Pope Francis, Supreme Pastor of the Church and most benevolent benefactor of our Order, each province shall celebrate one Mass.

For Pope Emeritus Benedict XVI, each province shall celebrate one Mass.

For fr. Bruno Cadoré, Master of the Order, each province shall celebrate one Mass.

For fr. Timothy Radcliffe and fr. Carlos A. Azpiroz Costa, ex- Masters of the Order, each province shall celebrate one Mass.

For the entire Episcopal Order, for the socii of the Master of the Order, for the Procurator General of the Order, for our benefactors and for the wellbeing of the entire Order of Preachers, each province shall celebrate one Mass.

Suffrages for the Dead

For the soul of Pope John Paul I each province shall celebrate one Mass. For the soul of fr. Damian Byrne, the most recently deceased Master of the Order, each province shall celebrate one Mass.

For the souls of the brothers and sisters of the Order who have died since the last General Chapter, each province should celebrate one solemn Mass for them all together.

When these prescribed suffrages, for either the living or the dead are to be fulfilled, they should be announced publicly and in sufficient time, so that the brethren of the convent where the suffrages are to be fulfilled can participate in the Mass celebrated for these intentions.

These are the Acts of the General Chapter of Priors Provincial of Bologna in Italy, celebrated in the convent of St. Dominic, from July 15 to August 4, of which the printed versions fixed with the seal of the Master of the Order ought to be applied with the same faith as the original text.

We command the superiors of all and each of the Provinces, convents and houses that the same acts be read as soon as possible in each of the convents and houses subject to them and to be published, and they should sedulously take care that they be observed by all.

In the name of the Father, and of the Son, and of the Holy Spirit.

Given in Bologna, in the convent of Holy Father Dominic, on August 4, in the year of our Lord 2016.

L. ⚜ S.

fr. Bruno Cadoré, OP
magister Ordinis

fr. Martin Ganeri , OP
prior provincialis provinciæ Angliæ

fr. Javier González Izquierdo, OP
prior provincialis provinciæ Dominæ Nostæ de Rosario

fr. Benjamin Sombel Sarr, OP
vice-provincialis vice-provinciæ S. Augustini in Africa occidentali

fr. Roberto Giorgis, OP
secretarius generalis capituli

fr. Gregorio Kim, OP
ab actis

Appendix I
Relatio on the State of the Order
to the General Chapter of Bologna in July 2016
Brother Bruno Cadoré op

"Proclaim the Word...
do the work of an evangelist...
fulfil your ministry" (2 Tim 4:2-5)

(1) In conformity with LCO 417 §II 3°, I present here a report on the
state of the Order with a view to the General Chapter of prior provincials which is to be celebrated at Bologna from July 16th to August
4th, 2016, at the heart of the Jubilee Year of the confirmation of the
Order: "You are sent to preach the gospel." In this perspective I shall
divide my *Relatio* into three parts. The first part will give an account
of the different *processes of restructuring* which have been carried
out in the course of the last few years with the aim of giving us more
energy for preaching by means of an improved synergy between the
structures, the life of the brethren, and the mission. The second part
is tied to *the life of the brothers and the communities* and its close
links with mission, the links by which we seek to witness to Him
who "went about doing good" (Acts 10:38). The third part will
discuss preaching and its many forms. I shall try to identify the
major issues of the ministry of *preaching in the service of the renewal
of evangelization* to which the celebration of the Jubilee is inviting
us – the Jubilee which in fact is to come to an end with the Congress
for the Mission of the Order.

(2) The General Chapter of Trogir asked for a commission to be set up to
evaluate the methods by which the work of General Chapters is
organized (ACG Trogir 2013 184). One of its recommendations was
**to *strengthen and improve the time of preparation for the
Chapter.*** For this reason, I shall allow myself, in the course of this
Relatio, to indicate the recurring themes and questions which have
surfaced during my visits and those of the socii in recent years. My
wish is twofold, first that this report may be an element from which
the Chapter is prepared in the provinces and communities, and
second, that this preparation will allow the Chapter to attend to the
major questions which brothers would like to see more fully
addressed. To round off this *Relatio,* the capitulars will receive an

account (cf. the Chapter's website) of how the guidance and decisions of Trogir have been followed up.

(3) May the Lord accompany us in this time of preparation for the Chapter, in such a way that at the heart of the celebration of the Jubilee it may be a moment when the two dimensions of evangelization confided to the Order by Pope Honorius III may be strengthened and confirmed (Bull of 21 January 1217): the evangelization of ourselves, and the evangelization of our ministry of the Word in the worlds of our time.

"To restructure for the sake of the preaching"

(4) The work of renewal which marks the period of the Jubilee has involved every one of us. Indeed, we are well aware that its objective is not simply to "restructure" institutions, provinces and communities, but rather to arrive at the structural changes that can make us freer and more available to be sent "joyfully and faithfully to proclaim the gospel of peace," guided by the Spirit of the Risen Christ (cf. the prayer for the Jubilee).

Statistics of the Order

(5) The following table gives the figures which show the changes in numbers of the Order and the Dominican Family in the course of the last three years.

Year end of	2012	2013	2014	2015 ?
Friars (all)	5955	5903	5826	
Priests	4430	4396	4355	
Deacons	67	90	76	
Bishops	36	37	36	
Cooperator bros	345	340	322	
Students	869	853	836	
Novices	208	187	201	
Died	109	111	98	
Extra conventum	333	346	308	
Exclaustration	84	90	68	
Dispensation from the Order – Simple Professed	54	39	48	
Dispensation from the Order – Solemn Professed	8	10	10	
Dispensation from the Priesthood – Deacons	3	1	2	
Dispensation from the Priesthood – Clerical friars	7	4	10	
Incardination into Diocese - Complete	9	1	7	
Incardination into Diocese - "*ad experimentum*"	5	2	5	
Number of priories	259	258	261	
Number of houses	333	314	316	
Average age			56 years	
Deceased Brothers	109	111	98	
Nuns	2773		2776	
Monasteries	219		202	
Apostolic Sisters	24,296		23,038	
Congregations	150		149	
Laity	166,000			
Secular Institutes	150			
Priestly fraternities	265		275	

(6) What have we to learn from these figures?
- We note a certain erosion of numbers. The impulse provided by the Jubilee might invite us to improve and reinforce our pastoral policy for vocations.

- In the course of the year 2014, 142 brothers made profession, 98 brothers died, and 77 brothers left the Order, most of them during the time of simple profession, but some of them later, and in particular, in order to seek for incardination into a diocese. This quite high number of brothers asking to leave the Order invites us constantly to evaluate and clarify our criteria for the discernment of vocations and the way we accompany the brethren during their primary formation and the years immediately following.
- The age profile of the brothers differs with the provinces. The average age shows that it will be important to get a more precise idea of the dynamic of the demography of the whole of the Order and of the regions.
- We have to note a certain disparity between the numbers of friars and the pace of their replacement. The five most populous provinces are *Hispania* (490), Poland (439), Vietnam (366), St. Joseph in the United States (309), and France (306). The five provinces with most student brothers are Vietnam (82), St. Joseph in the United States (67), Nigeria (63), Poland (53), and the Philippines (42).
- There are in the Order 261 priories and 316 houses, so there are more communities where the superior is nominated and not elected in the way that priors are. This inevitably has its consequences for the life of the provinces, the dynamics of chapters, both provincial and conventual, and the application in practice of the democracy that is dear to us. It affects the makeup and the dynamics of provincial chapters.
- Quite a large number of brothers live *extra conventum* (5%) and that should encourage us not to be resigned to situations which ought to remain the exception.
- We do not really have available to us a study of the profile by age of the monasteries which might help make better preparation for the future.
- Seven brothers have been appointed bishop since the Trogir Chapter: brothers Jorge Salidas, Giovanni Pazmino, David Martinez de Aguirre, David Macaire, Youssouf Mirkis, Carlos Azpiroz Costa, and Lorenzo Piretto.

Restructuring and Mission

(7) The General Chapter of Rome (2010) engaged the Order in a process of appraisal and restructuring which concerned in the first place the provinces and vicariates – general, regional and provincial – and also the institutions that are placed under the jurisdiction of the Master of the Order. Included in the process were the links of communication and solidarity within the Order. In all these fields, the perspective in view is to achieve the best possible climate for a synergy between the life of the communities and the mission, the evangelical and the apostolic life.

Provinces and Vicariates

(8) This is the perspective that has guided the work that has been carried out with each of the ten general vicariates which existed in 2010. Three of them have been, or are to be, declared vice provinces: St Thomas Aquinas in Belgium, Ecuador, and the Democratic Republic of Congo. The change in status of the general vicariates of South Africa and Taiwan is as yet uncertain and a process of reflection together with the Curia is going on. Five vicariates have been suppressed and have seen their mission and their territory confided to the apostolic solicitude of a province: these are the Baltic countries, Hungary, Ukraine, Puerto Rico, and Chile.

I would like to add here some words of commentary on this process.

-(9) In the first place I wish to express my great admiration for the magnanimity with which the brothers involved, in the vicariates as in the provinces whose help has been asked, have faced up to this restructuring. Even if we are very conscious of the need to act, and of the disparity between the canonical status of the entity in question and the resources it actually has available for its task, it is still difficult and often painful to turn the page on the history that gave us birth and fostered our vocation. Certainly there have been difficult moments here and there, resistance even, but never blindness to realities or to the priority that must be given to seeking the common good of the preaching. Our common purpose has been to discover how we can provide ourselves with the best means of ensuring the presence and the preaching of the Order in these places and cultures: this must remain the aim now in the new layout.

-(10) We have also been led to adjust the processes to local realities. This was the case, for example, for the establishment of the vicariate in Ukraine: after an assessment with the brethren, it seemed more appropriate to separate the house of St Petersburg from the vicariate and entrust it to the province of Poland as a house outside its own territory. Indeed, it seemed that this separation made it more possible to take account of the special characteristics of the two places so as to fit the preaching of the Order to them. Otherwise it leaves open the question of a possible larger deployment of our presence in Russia when the time comes. Two entities can be declared vice provinces according to the conditions laid down in LCO, but it seems important to set up a process of companionship and appraisal so as to be able to be sure, as the years go by, about how they are consolidating their position in a way that favors the mission. The Baltic countries have not been immediately erected as a provincial vicariate by the province of France, so as to leave time to measure the way their equilibrium and their synergies develop between the three presences in these territories, before we decide on the most suitable structures.

-(11) The new province called *Hispania* was erected in January 2016, uniting the three provinces that there were in Spain. It celebrated its first chapter in January, under the presidency of the first prior provincial who was instituted after consultation with all the brothers. This is the fruit of a patient and rigorous preparation, and it is to be accompanied by reorganization of the provincial vicariates of the new province. There will be a single vicariate of Cuba and San Domingo. We shall pursue the process of founding a vice province in Venezuela by merging its communities with the vicariate of the Rosary province. The province of Peru is moving towards taking charge of the apostolic vicariate of Puerto Maldonato. The regional vicariate of the province of the Rosary in Spain has chosen not to be part of the new province, and needs to agree on its precise relationship with the province of Hispania in the territory on which it is established. It should identify and formalize the way it collaborates with other entities in the whole of the Iberian Peninsula.

-(12) The province of Flanders, at the request of the provincial council, has been suppressed. Its priories and houses have been confided to the apostolic solicitude of the vice province of St Thomas Aquinas in Belgium, which has set up a provincial vicariate on this territory of Flanders. There again, if this decision has been painful, it has seemed to everyone to be the one best adapted to the situation, not only to manage the present state of affairs but also to make the best preparation for the future. This brave new departure seems to me to open up very interesting possibilities.

-(13) Certain provincial vicariates, due to their very small size, have been or ought to be suppressed and become overseas presences of a home province. This includes Belarus, Turkey, Slovenia, Bética in Venezuela, the Rosary in Taiwan, Grenada, Trinidad, etc. New vicariates should be set up in time to come, for example the Solomon Islands and Papua. In the same way, in conformity with LCO, the rights of this province and that have to be adjusted in the future. The Rosary province has engaged in a process of reflection with the Curia around the changes in legislation that are to be foreseen.

-(14) These reorganizations lead me to put a concern of mine to the Chapter. If I think it was necessary to proceed to these changes, I also think that the mission of preaching in these territories and cultures is most important for the whole of the mission of the Order, from the fact of the special linguistic or cultural character of a country, the history of a region, the balance of societies, existing or latent conflicts, the inter-religious context and so on. So it seems to me indispensable to spell out how the outlook, the experiences and the apostolic concern shared by our brothers, and by the Dominican family, in these vicariates are to be really represented within the general chapters and in the apostolic concern of all of us. Indeed, it seems to me that we have to find ways of strengthening the "missionary" dimension of the Order, against the temptation to fall back on the entities that are already established on the grounds of the scarcity of their resources.

- -(15) This concern came up in the sequel to the meeting in 2014 of those vicar-provincials and prior provincials concerned by these matters. We learnt a great deal from this encounter and it stressed the importance of these places of mission and/or of new foundations. In particular, the meeting drew attention to relations between a vicariate and its province in terms of the exchange of information, regular meetings of the vicariate council with the provincial council, the precise definition of fields of subsidiarity, clarity about the matters with which the prior provincial (as the sole major superior) intends to entrust the vicar provincial, and the furtherance of knowledge of the vicariate amongst the student brothers of the province. The same meeting also identified subjects to which the General Chapter should give its attention, for example to determine the essential elements that should be included in vicariate statutes (cf. LCO 384 b), and to recast the priorities for a mission "to the frontiers." The Chapter could give indications about how to take matters forward.

-(16) Our reflection on these entities of the Order serves to underline the importance the perspective of "mission" should have in the shared consciousness of all the brethren and the provinces of the Order. In this regard we should emphasize the way most of our present vicariates are situated in places which are very important for the global dynamics of today: the world of Islam, Cuba, the secularized countries, seats of conflict like the Central African Republic, Democratic Republic of Congo, Rwanda Burundi and Ukraine, regions where the future presents challenges – Flanders in Belgium, South Africa, Dacia, the Baltic states, Hungary, etc. I think we have still to improve the spreading of information, and reaction to that information, about these places in the Order as a whole. This "solidarity in concern" gives a further spur to the building of unity amongst us. It seems to me that the question of solidarity and the specific ways (not only economic) we put it into action, should be taken up by the Chapter.

-(17) The restructuring process makes us feel the importance of the value we give to the missionary dimension of the provinces. In this sense several provinces have been, or will be, asked to explore the possibility of making new foundations, as is the case for Nigeria in Zambia, whoever we can find for Madagascar, and perhaps we should also explore the needs of eastern Europe.

Institutions under the immediate jurisdiction of the Master of the Order

(18) During the last three years the restructuring process has also concerned the institutions placed under the immediate jurisdiction of the Master of the Order. The chapter of Trogir made a number of recommendations about this (see ACG Trogir 2013 97-105), and I set out here the main lines of the work undertaken there, so as to be clear about how the Bologna Chapter needs to assess it.

-(19) *Angelicum* Once its new University Statutes were approved on June 26th, 2014, an Administrative Council was put in place together with a program for the restoration of the fabric, a distinction being made between the premises of the university and those of the community. The management of the patrimony and of the capital was reorganized. It is understood that this reorganization has to accompany the work done by the academic Senate and the council of every Faculty so as to express in their main lines the academic aims of teaching and research. In this option, I propose to consider the following aspects:

- o The Angelicum is our university presence in Rome and the place to which numerous clergy, lay people and religious come from abroad to receive all or part of their formation. We give an important service to the universal Church by developing the recruitment and the welcome given these students, and by offering them the education that reflects the Dominican tradition both in method and in content. To do this we should do more to turn to account the pastoral links and the resources of research and teaching of the Order as a whole.
- o Being present in Rome, the Angelicum could be, even more than it is presently, the place where in a regular and organized way, the different research centers of the Order

would offer the fruit of their work, either as postgraduate seminars, or as regular sessions of ongoing formation open to all students present in Rome. I am thinking for example of our resources in biblical studies, Thomist studies, the interreligious dialogue, knowledge of Islam, expertise in social studies, etc.

o It seems to me that the bilingual character of the University is an advantage we should maintain so as to allow students to benefit from the universal resources of the Order.

o Student brothers of the Order who come to the Angelicum always emphasize how valuable this experience of universality is for them. Could we not make it a major objective for the Dominican Family?

o The faculties need a strong nucleus of teaching staff engaged in research including the brothers and the Sisters – whose presence needs to be expanded – and lay people who really can carry forward the academic project of each faculty. It seems to me that it should be possible to do this by making the Angelicum part of a dynamic of exchanges and collaboration, to last for an agreed period, between the Order's centers of study.

-(20) There needs to be some forward planning about the *Convitto* of the Angelicum and the apostolic objective we are aiming for, to support priests in formation who come from dioceses with slender means and to share in forming leaders and pastors of young Churches. If we decide to go in this direction we have to ask whether we have the means to do this in the long term, and whether a clearer synergy with the Angelicum could be developed, and also how the *Convitto* can strengthen the links of this or that province with its local Church.

-(21) *The French School of Biblical and Archaeological Studies at Jerusalem.* Here again, after steps were taken to assess the situation, new Statutes were presented to the Congregation for Catholic Education which confirmed them on September 10th, 2013. Furthermore, a process of renewal of the body of teachers-researchers is being undertaken. I wish here to thank the provinces which have been asked to help in this renewal. Here again, allow me to express some suggestions for the future, taking into account all that I have been able to observe in recent years:

- o   It seems to me very meaningful that the Order of Preachers be able to develop the influence of the School as a center for research and teaching of the Word, and very important that this be done in collaboration with everyone, and on the spot, with other institutions of the same kind.
- o   Three perspectives, it seems to me, should be given priority: implementing the program of work of the newly formed team, consolidating the research project the *Bible in Its Traditions* (BEST), and greater involvement of the Order in the archaeological project.
- o   The School might eventually become a privileged place where a time of study of the Word could be offered to all the student brothers of the Order at some point in their course.
- o   In the present context, I believe that a proposal by the school on the theme "Word and Theology" as a service to the Order and to the Church would make a good deal of sense, especially in the world of faculties of theology and seminaries. This could be one more useful field of collaboration.

-(22) *The Historical Institute of the Order:* a new director has been appointed together with a council. They are to work along the lines given by the new statutes dated September 21st,2015. A more organic link is still to be developed with the Archives of the Order and those of the provinces. The Institute should also propose, encourage and support research projects in the field of the history of the Order (and at the present time, for example, projects about the history of the Lay Dominicans and that of Cooperator Brothers in the Order). The Jubilee Year puts its emphasis on the way our creativity in evangelization draws strength and inspiration from the study of our history.

-(23) *The Leonine Commission* is also to renew its Statutes so as to adapt itself to the contemporary world of research, in which it is successfully holding its own, for example by securing the collaboration of lay people. One important milestone has been the publication of the Sermons of Thomas within the last few years. We need still to find how to reinforce the team of researchers and prepare brothers to join it.

-(24) Work remains to be done on the mission of *the College of St. Mary Major.* For this service of the Church we need to form a college of twelve confessors. Presently two ordinary and one extraordinary confessor are lacking. Furthermore, it seems to me that we should form confessors in advance, for example by asking certain provinces to prepare brothers to join the college for a specified period, say five years. Once again this means asking brothers to leave their province for a time, which it seems is more and more difficult to do. This is why it seems to me that we have to reach a decision about it. I think that if we can't take collective responsibility for such a very Dominican ministry of mercy according to the demands of the Holy See, and replace the confessors regularly, it would be fairer to entrust it to others. I have recently written to prior provincials along these lines.

-(25) The *Priory of the Albertinum* is pursuing its mission by strengthening its relations and its collaboration with the Priory of St. Hyacinth (ACG Trogir 2013 101). But following the work of the commission set up at the request of the Trogir Chapter it appeared not to be the right time to think of uniting the two Priories.

-(26) I leave it to the Socius for the Life of Study to give an account of the links with the Universities (in particular, Manila) and the Faculties (Fribourg amongst others) of which the Master is the Grand Chancellor, a responsibility which takes different forms in different cases.

-(27) *The International Liturgical Commission* has been renewed in the course of the last three years. On the basis of its Report it would be useful if the Chapter would give directions about its priorities for the next three years.

Solidarity

(28) Another process of reorganization concerns Solidarity, with the setting up of the service *Spem Miram* led by a commission of five brothers and chaired by Br. Dominic Izzo. In my letter entitled *Beggars standing by one another* of May 24th,2014 I emphasized the challenge of promoting amongst us a new "culture of solidarity": I believe this links very directly with the mission of preaching. Concerning solidarity, one aspect is obviously the pooling of the resources that are available to support projects put forward by the brethren. But more broadly the development of the activities of *Spem Miram* should progressively help us take joint responsibility for a number of apostolic projects. And if I may insist, not only to put up new buildings but also to set up working parties and make meetings possible. Another task is to lessen the divide which exists between entities, in particular where it concerns primary formation, further studies and the formation of the formators.

(29) My visits to the Order have indeed given me the conviction that a priority of our solidarity today concerns primary formation, in order that together we may provide our new brothers with the conditions and the time which are necessary for study. From this point of view, I wish the Chapter to give clear directives, and that we put our shoulder to the task.

(30) The funds available for solidarity being still quite limited, we have until now confined the help we give to the brothers and the nuns. We are in discussion with the sisters of apostolic life to see how we might help them to take steps to put in place a similar system amongst themselves. No doubt our limited resources should spur us to improve fundraising for the whole of the Order.

(31) *The International Dominican Foundation* has pursued its mission during these three years, and one director has given place to his successor. I thank them both for their generous service. Here again we have had to match the means to the ends, particularly in distributing study grants. It seems to me that the allocation of these grants could be the principal object of the IDF, following the coordination that is developing between the centers of study of

the Order and the institutions under the immediate jurisdiction of the Master of the Order.

Media

(32) Throughout these six years the service of the Media has also been reorganized. First of all, a new website for the Order and its Newsletter was set up along with a network of correspondents in the provinces. The aim is that the site may be increasingly seen by us all as the place in which we can exchange information. I note that it is still difficult to keep up the flow of information between the provinces and the Order's website, though it could become an important force of the unity of the Order and lift us out of provincialism.

(33) This restructuring of communications has also involved putting in place an internal system of communication in the Order, including the work of the Curia itself, with networks to facilitate the work of institutions – links between provincial priors and regents of study, etc. – and forums for preaching and networks for the apostolate. We are now at a stage where it becomes necessary to strengthen the "professional" team so as to use our technical potential to the full. For this we need both a team of technical professionals and the engagement – full-time or on a short-term basis – of experts in the social media. Indeed, I think that with the help of such a team of professionals it would be possible to offer training in this area to the brothers and Sisters of the Order and so promote the involvement of brothers in this new form of preaching in their province. The opening of the Jubilee has given us the occasion to consolidate the external communications of the Order, in particular in the social networks, and we are becoming more aware of ways in which we might encourage cooperation with the laity and so improve our evangelizing mission. It is for the Chapter to give guidance on this for the coming years.

Apostolic Life

(34) Preparing for the Congress for the Mission of the Order which is to round off the Jubilee Year leads me to think that it could be useful to put in place a more organized body to give leadership to the apostolic life of the whole of the Order, a "secretariat for the Apostolic Life," that would be the responsibility of the Socius for

the Apostolic Life. Indeed, we have come to a moment when we could usefully strengthen the synergies between different projects, bodies and initiatives, in particular:

-(35) With the apostolic priorities of the Order and the Dominican Family in mind, the approaching Congress should identify themes and lines of approach to help the Order discern how it may best assist the renewal of evangelization in the Church. It's a matter of finding the means to pursue this work, with an emphasis on the connection between theology and pastoral care.

-(36) Our thinking should help to identify the apostolic partnerships that can develop between the provinces and the new missions and foundations the Order may open. The Secretariat for Apostolic Life will be responsible for following this up, and for helping the Order to keep alive its "thirst for mission."

-(37) From this viewpoint, and in cooperation with the relevant Promoters of the laity, the nuns, the rosary, the media, Justice and Peace, and the members of the international desk of the Dominican Family, we must receive concrete suggestions for joint initiatives amongst the different branches of the Family. Emphasizing this in our common mission will illustrate the special character which the "Dominican family" dimension can give to the preaching of the Order today.

-(38) The promotion of Justice and Peace and of Care for Creation must be at the heart of these synergies. The priority must be to establish a structural link between this promotion on the ground – in the concrete situations to which provincial and regional promoters can bear witness – and the work of the permanent delegation of the Order to the UN in Geneva but also in New York, and progressively in the other places where the UN is present, e.g. Vienna, Paris and Nairobi.

-(39) In this perspective the "Salamanca process" (ACG Trogir 2013 112-114) is of special importance. It aims to establish the connection between apostolic engagement in situations where human rights are denied, and theological and interdisciplinary reflection. In the context of the Jubilee a conference has been planned to open up the theme and promote this process. While it answers to the concerns of many people, and corresponds to the realities with which the preaching of the Order is confronted, it is slow to get off the ground. I propose that the Chapter should specify a development plan for it and indicate the criteria and the time frame by which it is to be assessed.

-(40) The Media Service should obviously have an important part to play in this plan of action, both as concerns the promotion of communities and the networks that allow them to work together, and with regard to apostolic inventiveness and the partnerships to which preaching to the "new digital continent" call us.

-(41) A "commission for the apostolic life" could find its place in supporting this new service, regularly enriching its work with testimony from the diversity, in diverse latitudes and cultures, of the preaching of the Order and of the Dominican family.

-(42) To me it seems most important that this work of realizing the synergies should be accompanied by a close collaboration with the commission for the intellectual life, in such a way that the apostolic life and theology should always be in a close dialogue.

Consolidating collaborations

(43) In the wake of all this restructuring I would like the Chapter to seek to put in place the structures and dynamics of collaboration between the provinces, something essential for the future. Three areas seem to me to have priority:

-(44) *Primary formation* to begin with, and this at three levels. First, we have to recognize that certain provinces are in real financial difficulty in providing primary formation and the formation of the formators. How can collaboration, exchanges, regular financial support, a fund set up for the whole Order, remedy this iniquitous state of affairs? There again, primary formation is certainly the period when the Order has every interest in organizing exchanges between provinces, in such a way that new brothers in their first years in the Order get the chance to discover other sides to the Order and other cultures of the Church, the Order, and its apostolate and intellectual life. Lastly this sort of collaboration would doubtless allow of regrouping of efforts between provinces, the better to take on the responsibility of forming preachers for the Order, while retaining sufficient energy for apostolic creativeness.

-(45) *Encouraging apostolic collaboration* by promoting the exchange of assignationsbetween provinces – assignations to missionary projects outside one's own province, with a view to the good of the whole Order. This is, and is going to be, particularly important if we want to strengthen the kind of especially significant presences that a province may find it hard to maintain all by itself. These may be missions: to give a few examples, Turkey, Albania, Amazonia, Verapaz and Chiapas, Indonesia, South Africa Then there are the more classic apostolates that are essential to us but fragile, for example, universities, centers of study, important town centers and so on. From this point of view, I would like us to take time to consider the usefulness of assigning a brother "in the mode of Providence," both with regard to the brother himself and to the life of the communities and the provinces. Previously such assignations have opened the door to doing jobs together here and there. But nowadays they are more likely to run the risk of a mismatch between the individual position of brothers who are assigned in this way and the apostolic mission of the priory, given the responsibility it has with regard to the planning of the life and mission of the province as a whole.

-(46) If this meets with the support of the Chapter, I am thinking of launching a study on the question of establishing *a better synergy between the centers of teaching and research of the provinces,* and also between those centers and *the institutions under the immediate jurisdiction of the Master of the Order.* On the one hand this would add an international and intercultural dimension to the qualifications of our teachers and researchers, and, if need be, would improve the path to better accreditation. Moreover, it would help us to really integrate all the institutions into the common dynamic of the Order's life of study. We have in view assignations made for a set period but which fit into the dynamics of a path to qualification. This will favor a free flow between institutions instead of a competition for scarce resources.

The Dominican Family: an appeal to give pride of place to collaborations

(47) Right from the beginning, St. Dominic's intuition attracted men and women to come together from their different states of life, religious, lay people and priests. Ever since, as the centuries have passed, and specially with the development of the Third Order, very many congregations of Sisters of apostolic life and the arrival of Secular Institutes have enriched the Dominican Family. Today in times when there is talk in the Church of "new spiritual families" the heirs and heiresses of the "holy preaching of Prouille" are being challenged to carry that preaching forward in the service of the renewal of evangelization. I would like the International Bureau of the Dominican Family to help the Master of the Order to promote it, along the lines that the Chapter will indicate. This important dimension of the life of the Order must become part and parcel of the process of restructuring for our preaching.

(48) Visitations to the Order are very often occasions to rejoice in the riches of the *different branches of the Dominican Family,* their influential witness of their apostolates and the fraternal friendship which for the most part marks their relationships with one another. But very often this thankfulness comes with the desire to see more synergy and collaboration in common projects develop, and a united, well-designed and distinctive contribution to the Church's evangelizing mission. Clearly what is needed in the first place is a growth in our knowledge and mutual regard for one another. We have to consult together and identify the needs of the Church and the world to which the charism of the Order chiefly needs to respond. We must grow a spirit of humility to lead us to rejoice in one another's preaching before we start comparing ourselves or even competing! There already exist many joint initiatives. The *Lectio Divina* project is a good example, and the many ways in which we preach the Rosary, and we should develop this more. I have often had the occasion in these years to give the

field of education as an example, concerning as it does young people and their families. It's a field where the Dominican Family with its kindergartens, schools, colleges and universities has much to give. We have plenty of good reasons for thinking that the tradition of the Order has its specific contribution to give to education. But these days this field is also undergoing extensive changes, and in many places religious institutions are dispossessed of their role in education and see their future put in question. I realize that too often we are not taking thought and working together so as to anticipate and secure the future of this service. We run the risk that it will all sadly disappear in the end.

(49) *The cloistered nuns of the Order* are at the heart of this "holy preaching." Here I would like to express a profound thanksgiving for their presence in the Order and the witness of their vocation, and my deepest gratitude for the support they bring to the preaching of the Order. Here again an extensive reordering is necessary and is presently being pursued. New monasteries are opening in Benin, Bolivia, Vietnam, and Zambia, and other plans are being discussed. There is a process of closing and merging houses in certain countries where there are too many monasteries for the number of new vocations, today chiefly in Spain and in Italy. More fundamentally may I draw attention to current reflection begun on the initiative of the Congregation for the Institutes of Consecrated Life and the Societies of Apostolic Life. Starting from an inquiry that has been carried out in every monastery of the universal Church, the Holy See wants to open up discussion on the themes of the autonomy of monasteries, primary formation, the Federations, and where appropriate, the links with the male branches of each Institute. On the basis of this inquiry, whose returns are now being opened, the Holy Father will be asked for an "*aggiornamento*" of the texts which regulate the monastic life of women in the Church, and in particular papal enclosure. The monasteries of the Order have as their particular feature a direct and regular bond with the Master of the Order. On this account theirs is a distinctly original position in comparison with all the rest. I believe that the place of the monasteries at the very heart of the unity of the Order for eight centuries is of great moment in giving firm foundation to the ministry of itinerant preaching. If this reform is put in place, and if the nuns [*moniales]* are in agreement, we must make sure that their special character

is respected and promoted. For my part I think that the nuns [*moniales*] are not to be thought of first of all as the Dominican way of belonging to all the various monastic traditions of the Church. Rather it is the case that in founding them Dominic wanted the monastic way to be at the heart of the "holy preaching," and that invites us all the more to strengthen our unity, respecting of course the specific character of this life and the structure proper to a monastery in the Church.

(50) In many provinces the *Lay Dominican Fraternities* are benefiting from a renewal of their membership and also from the dynamism that makes them fully part of the mission of the Order. It makes us very happy to see the Order opening up the riches of its charism like this so as to foster the lay calling and mission in the Church. But it is also an appeal to a greater responsibility: how can we develop even more fully, and in a more defined, regular and structured way, the union of the lay vocation, the religious vocation of women, and the religious and priestly vocation of the brothers, into one single mission of evangelization? Or to put it another way, in this precise moment in the history of the Church, how are the lay people of the Order going to exercise their own calling to preach the gospel at the heart of the particular church community to which they belong, but also in the universal perspective of the mission of the Order? And if it is to find an echo, how will the men and women religious of the Order welcome their contribution, encourage and accompany it where necessary, and learn from it? The links between local, national and international levels deserve clearer definition. Apart from this, it seems to me that too often we consider the reality of the Dominican Laity under the aspect of their individual commitments, without including their families in the picture. We should take more account of that, especially in the light of the recommendations of the recent Synod of bishops. It would be a good time to pursue an international shared reflection among the laity of the Order on the different ways of becoming involved as a family in the spreading of the gospel. That would be a great gift to the whole Order.

(51) After a period of appraisal we have undertaken to relaunch *Dominican Volunteers International*, which should provide a fine space for collaboration within the Dominican Family.

(52) I am particularly happy with the development of the *Dominican Youth Movement;* whose new Statutes are to be presented to the Chapter. It seems obvious to me that today more than ever, evangelization needs to vary its forms and its language. The IDYM opens up this possibility, especially where it concerns conversation ("the visit of the gospel") with the younger generation which in every clime and culture now tends to distance itself from the Church. It had to be structured realistically so that cultural diversity could be taken into account, so that the methods of organization might be light and pliable enough, that it should enjoy the right kind of autonomy that would respect young people's own particular commitment and the close link with other branches. Important steps have been taken. I sometimes regret that with us, as with the Church in general, it is so difficult to give "the youth" a real place as actors in evangelizing and not just that of recipients, however privileged, of our pastoral care.

(53) On the subject of the laity in the Dominican Family, I would like to draw attention to the dynamism of the many groups of laity who are associated with one or another Congregation of apostolic Sisters, or with a priory of the brethren. In addition, I can point to the *groups and associations* now appearing, especially of young people and particularly engaged in evangelization under new forms, for example the digital social networks and the arts. They would like to be more closely associated with the Order. This could certainly play a big role in enriching our common preaching. The *Dominican Secular Institutes* presently remain quite few and fragile, but the special character of their vocation should certainly retain our attention at a time when "secularization" is so much talked about.

(54) The *Dominican Priestly Fraternities* presently enjoy a promising development which we must continue to encourage (ACG Trogir 2013 20). This is certainly a very original way of putting the charism of the Order at the service of the life of the diocesan churches. In my reflection on the contribution of the Order to the local Church which will form the third chapter of this *Relatio,* it is right to emphasize how the Fraternities can offer new opportunities for collaboration and also improve understanding between a local Church and the Order.

(55) Finally, the dynamism of many *congregations of apostolic Sisters* gives me joy when I visit them, and also the diversity and richness of the apostolic and evangelical witness of the congregations. These days they are more marked by age and by a kind of uncertainty about the future. I am very conscious that neither the Master of the Order nor a General Chapter should meddle in the lives of the apostolic congregations. However, precisely in my role as Master of the Order, I must express my particular concern that the Sisters of apostolic life might together discover how to secure the future of this specific vocation within the "holy preaching," for this is a need for all of us. I also think it is important that the brothers take care not to take initiatives in these matters except in strict collaboration with the Sisters. Without pretending that this is a final truth, I believe that the future should not go the way of scattering the Sisters, and that it is for the Sisters themselves to determine the forms in which, having taken into consideration all the factors – social and cultural change, economic and social progress, the change in the status of women in society and in the Church, the Sisters of St. Dominic are called on to evangelize. I also think that the Master of the Order must seriously reflect with the Sisters about the criteria and the limits of new affiliations and aggregations so as not to increase the dispersion even more.

"The Life and Mission of the brothers and the communities"

(56) The celebration of the Jubilee of the confirmation of the Order invites us to remember that St. Dominic in dealing with Pope Honorius III laid great stress on his brothers receiving the name of "preachers." They were not to be described by the acts of preaching they might perform: it was rather that preaching should determine their lives to the point of becoming its very identity. The "life of the friar preacher," individually and in community, holds together contemplative prayer and praise, and preaching. It is the vector of transmission in preaching of the superabundance ofcontemplation.

The life of the communities

(57) This interaction of contemplation and preaching can be a useful standpoint from which to describe the life of the communities of the Order. It is in this sense that we may understand the invitation,

recently repeated, to each priory that it should engage in a process of formulating the apostolic plans of the community.

More often than not the communities are doing well, it seems to me. However, I would like to mention in this Report the questions or difficulties that keep coming up in the course of the visitations.

(58) *Dialogue and communication between the brothers* in many communities is found to be insufficient, fragile and in some cases, alas, almost non-existent. In consequence communication and the exchange of information are often very weak, so that the community becomes a collection of individuals thrown together instead of a place where mutual support and encouragement help each brother fulfil his humanity as a believer and develop his vocation as a preacher. Sometimes this leads one brother or another to develop his own network of friendship and solidarity, and this becomes a more important point of reference than one's own community. Let me emphasize a commonplace finding in most provinces: the brothers just like every human being need to be supported and recognized in their lives and their commitments. Very often when I am told that such and such a brother is never there or does not get involved in the community, I realize that this brother – who no doubt has his own failings and his own responsibility in the matter – is looking outside for the recognition that he doesn't find (but perhaps he is wrong to think that) within his own community. This question of being recognized, which reinforces our confidence in our identity, is, it seems to me, an essential part of the way we live in community and the way our communities are led. When I have to examine (alas!) requests to leave the Order so as to be incardinated in a diocese, I often ask myself whether one of the motives of such requests isn't precisely that these brothers receive the recognition they look for more from their function as pastors than they do from their own community or province. Priors and superiors should have a care to promote the recognition of each of the brothers, and so should formators whose ministry it is to help each one fulfil his capacities.

(59) On the subject of communication in communities, I am struck when it comes home to me how sometimes it is so hard for the brothers to *be reconciled* to one another. Sometimes, tensions, conflicts, jealousies, and animosities between individuals make life harder

for everyone. The General Chapter of Trogir called on communities to confront the facts and to get into the habit of celebrating reconciliation among the brethren. It is an appeal which remains relevant today.

(60) In this field of communication, visitations quite often show that each community can have *the tendency to a certain "isolationism"* or self-centeredness, giving little attention to the provincial plan for the mission (see below). This sometimes gives the impression that for each community the important thing is to keep going, without giving much attention to the province as a whole or to its apostolic plans. Sometimes they even seem not to know much about the life of other communities or indeed the universal life of the Order. This underlines the need to promote the exchange of information, but also of visits. It also shows how communities and provinces in the Order could benefit from exchanges and reciprocal assignations between the provinces. In making up communities, care should be taken to foster the international and intercultural aspects.

(61) With regard to the life of the brethren, special mention should be made of the *more elderly brothers* among us. Though in many places we can report that they receive much attention, generosity and inventiveness so as to ensure the best possible relations between generations, including support for those who need it and skilled assistance with their problems of health, there are cases where this reality is still neglected or even ignored (or denied). Evidently we cannot prescribe solutions that will be valid for every place and culture, ones that will best make growing old a part of our life. However, the human, religious, apostolic and spiritual concerns that this represents, both for older brothers and for younger ones, call on us to make this an essential theme as we work on our plans for the life and mission of the provinces.

(62) *The place of contemplation and of the regular celebration of the Liturgy of the Hours* as the source of fraternal communion among us, with the care given to its quality and its beauty – the beauty of the place and of the chant – seems to me in some places too easily reduced to the minimum that is required in terms of time (saying the Office as fast as possible), regularity, and beauty. Often, and especially in the smaller communities, first place is given to the

program of celebrations in the parish or priory church and in various communities of religious – with as a result, a small number of Eucharistic celebrations for the community. I think we would profit from considering what this dimension brings to our regular life, and to the quality of both our life in community and our personal lives, besides the witness which the choral dimension of our regular life adds to our preaching.

(63) I insist on this point because here and there and in every part of the world brothers frequently express the desire to strengthen the mystical and contemplative (which does not mean monastic) dimension of the life of the brethren and of the community. This dimension is surely essential for each of us, and it belongs to us all to promote the spirit of communion and of eschatological witness at the heart of our life. Our care must be that our community should be for each of us, and every day, the place of our own evangelization and our spiritual resourcing, just as it is the place of our commitment to a shared watchfulness over our vocation. To establish our communities as places of study and of contemplative preaching, "spaces of contemplation": this represents the need of the people to which our communities must strive to reply. It is no waste of time or energy to foster the conditions for the brethren to rejoice in the full flourishing of their vocation. But this also corresponds to an apostolic need which is very strong today, as it echoes the thirst of so many of our contemporaries to discover places and communities of contemplation and of wisdom.

(64) During visitations we notice the difficulties there can be in setting up a regular program of *conventual chapters, councils and community meetings.* Sometimes, we are told that chapters are simply places where information is given, or where decisions made elsewhere are recorded (ones made by the prior or superior by himself, or by the council which thus sees itself given a charge it shouldn't have). Whenever this happens, we can see that individual and subjective choices and opinions are taking the place of a concerted reference to our laws and their objective character. Still on this subject, the visits and consultations that turn up at Santa Sabina show that too often the knowledge of LCO is fairly weak, and sometimes interpretations are being made to suit a person's interest. This is to be regretted, for usually when

one tries to solve a problem or a difficult personal situation without a rigorous and objective reference to our laws, it provokes an insoluble imbroglio in the long term. What is at stake in government inspired by fraternal charity is always to hold mercy and justice together.

(65) In the same frame of reference of there being a common objective standard for the lives of the brethren and the communities, and for the apostolic courses they take, I want to emphasize here the importance we should advisedly give to the given points of reference for the apostolic responsibilities we share: the acts of the general and provincial chapters, the conclusions of canonical visitation of the priors provincial, and the minutes of conventual chapters. Once again if we overlook them we risk falling into the trap of subjectivism, and that is perhaps more to be feared than individualism.

(66) The statistics have shown how the number of houses is greater than the number of priories. It seems to me that it is really important to think about this phenomenon and its reasons and consequences. We also note that small communities pose particular questions in the matter of assignations (most frequently raising the problem of the balance of personalities), the matter of the balance between community life and apostolic activity, or again the presence of the apostolic intentions of a house in the provincial chapter. It seems to me that a reflection on the fact that our tradition is conventual would be particularly useful today.

(67) It appears to me that we should think more about *the function of the prior in the communities* and the manner in which they support him in the exercise of the charge which they have confided to him. In many places it seems harder and harder to find priors, and besides, it seems more and more difficult to exercise this ministry when the brothers expect of the prior that he should act as the manager who puts at everyone's disposition the best possible living conditions, while not being willing to accept that he exercises the function of superior in their respect – the one to whom they give an account of their activity and its financial side, and the one who is the final point of reference for decisions about apostolic commitments. He it is who ensures the service of unity, and who seeks to establish the most just balance between respect

for the subjective story of each brother and the common recourse of everyone to the same Constitutions.

(68)   Among the conventual "officers," *the conventual lector* should have his proper place, though in many communities he is missing. In the Order, study in common is a constitutive part of the establishment of our communities, and I encourage the communities and provinces to keep alive this priority of study in common. Certainly everybody (more or less) has occasion to study in his own field of interest and competence. However, to study together, to search the Scriptures together, to exchange reasoned positions on theological, ecclesiological and moral topics, forms the basis on which we build up our unity. And it is the task of the lector to promote the care for common study in the midst of the brethren. In a province, regular meetings of the lectors amongst themselves and with the priors can be a real help to giving ongoing formation all its importance.

(69)   All these remarks converge on the care we should all have for *democracy.* We like to say that the Order has the strength of a great democratic tradition, and I am convinced of this. Still it seems to me that in the Order, as in the world at large, we run the risk of a minimal sort of democracy limited to matching up majority and minority opinions, with the play between the two. As is often said, the democracy of the Order consists in a democratic search for unanimity. In other words, the shared perspective in favor of the common good, and the growth of communion between us, is the determining factor for our style of democracy. It cannot be reduced to the casting of votes; it must first take root in an authentic dialogue. This is what motivates the involvement of everyone, in actual practice and without reserve, in the life of our community, our vicariate, our province and our Order.

Community Project

(70)   In writing the letter asked of me on this subject, I sought to argue how this aspect of communal life and its particular ministry of witness to fraternal communion, draws together the apostolic commitments of each brother in the community in one act of preaching. In this community project, it is a question, in the end, of harnessing the identity of each brother and that of the community.

Without repeating the same letter, I would like to highlight three points.

(71) First, *the importance of evaluation* proposed in the light of priorities given to the Order in the course of General Chapters. I feel it goes without saying that, beginning from these priorities, it is a matter for each community to evaluate to what extent it can be "Dominican." The issue is rather to make sure that none of our communities departs from what the Order considers the stepping stones for all evangelization. And, from this point of view, how to cultivate from particular and local roots a vital link with the perspectives of the Order's universal preaching. On this precise point, the confirmation of the Order launched a universal mission of preaching. This articulates an irrefutable dimension of the work of preaching by the whole community: to create for the Church a vital link between particular and universal. This link is particularly essential with regard to the most exposed, fragile and broken places of the world.

(72) We have brothers and sisters in these places: migrants, indigenous populations, places of conflict of identity or nation, instability and marginalization produced by globalization. Recent questions raised by increasing cases of forced migration create a special call to focus attention on this link between particular and universal. Such a community is equipped to accommodate or contribute to the welcome of migrants from the Near East. We have brothers and sisters in this region: what links can we build with them? Very often, people forced to leave their country paradoxically become refugees in countries whose policies also share in one way or another the features which constrained them to leave their country: what initiative can we take in this regard, provoked by the need to listen to the voice of those who, so often, are marginalized into silence?

(73) The second aspect I want to emphasize is *itinerancy*, not only conceived as a "readiness to move," nor even simply accepting changes of assignation, but more fundamentally our personal and communal availability to be "uprooted" from our established positions and certainties. Such itinerancy, at once evangelical and apostolic, is about prioritizing through common reflection what we want to achieve and what we think we must preserve in

response to the needs of the Church and of the world. Too often we are actors, evaluators and decision-makers at the same time and this pushes us to find ways of "preserving" what we already have and do. This is true for apostolic tasks, our pastoral and sacramental services. But it is also true for those apostolic institutions that we preserve against all odds, even when, having been important, the situation suggests it no longer responds to a need (e.g. a journal, a conference center or center for spirituality, an educational institution). Such "preservation" is also true for the internal organization of a community with its rhythms, relationships and its explicit or implicit influence on members of the community. There are many current examples: the welcome of brothers from new generations, the promotion of interculturalism in our communities, regular renewal of a community, implementing a new preaching project, asking that the schedule be rethought, the rhythms and fraternal links, the place in the local church... While it is true that developing a community project is fundamentally how a community is responsible for "strengthening and confirming" the Order in a place, the work of appraisal and call to mobility that may come must follow consciously from the needs that must be met. What is the specific service that the Church has a right to expect from the "holy preaching"? How do we always give priority to people's needs and to the needs of the Church before looking to preserve at all costs what we often do well but not always in response to a real demand or necessity? We are itinerants the better to meet the needs of our time.

(74) The third aspect is the *process of recognition,* already mentioned above, by which personal and communal identities are asserted, secured and consolidated. In the course of my visits, I have come to emphasize that many of the difficulties encountered in the process of evaluation, assignation and invitation to mobility, would be alleviated by not ignoring the need for recognition in building up each brother's identity.

As I wrote in my letter, the development of a community project is the opportunity to stimulate in every brother the consolidation of his "identity as preacher." From this point of view, I think it is also the opportunity to approach questions of enculturation together, questions that happily are becoming more and more important with the changing makeup of the Order. How are the "characteristics of the Dominican life" to be given as much attention as the cultures of origin in this process of enculturation?

(75) Speaking of the community project, it is appropriate to emphasize *the importance for a province to develop its own common project* which, because it will be developed with the participation of all, would form the common base upon which to build the foundations and decisions for apostolic direction and assignation. *Provincial Chapters* should usually be the place for such development, or at least an essential point of reference in the process. In view of this, each province ought to consider how their chapters are prepared, celebrated, and received.

Formation

(76) The purpose of formation, we should say, is to form preachers, namely, men whose life will be shaped both by contemplation and preaching. We accept this responsibility with gratitude when we welcome the new vocations the Lord entrusts to the Order.

Initial formation

(77) Before dealing with some particular questions about initial formation, I would like to state once again the following conviction. Setting aside our satisfaction at the number of vocations or our concern in places where numbers currently decline, what is essential is that we continue to ask ourselves what the Lord wants us to say when he trusts us to send new friars to become preachers. Certainly, we should have thorough, demanding procedures for formation that allow young friars to learn the tradition of the Order, becoming full participants in the tradition and passing it on in their turn. But we should also embrace what these young friars bring to the Order and evaluate and modify these procedures. Here and there they come bringing new ideas. Most of them enter with previous formation that gives them a significant knowledge of contemporary culture (economy, industry, computing, new digital communication, natural sciences, social sciences...) By analogy, I think we should see this in the light of Dominic's gesture of sending friars to study in the University. If the Church is to hold a "conversation" with the world, the gift vocations represent should be that the Order

incorporate what these new friars bring into an interaction between study and preaching. Of course, entry into religious life represents a break, a call to detachment and change of direction: young friars aspire to this radicalism. But therefore in every place of initial formation we should consider part of this "radicalism" to be a call to continually renew our preaching and ensure that each friar acknowledge this wealth of formation (which led young men to the Order) as a fruitful contribution to renew our "contemplative study."

(78) In writing the new *Ratio Formationis Generalis*, the General Council wanted to prioritize a point frequently made at General Chapters: we want to form Friars Preachers. I am often appreciative of the efforts, generosity and patience with which provinces undertake initial formation and would like to express the Order's gratitude to all formators who do not stint in their efforts to "found the Order of Preachers every day" as Lacordaire said. Listening to the young brothers, I am also appreciative of their generosity which very often leads them to give up future projects, personal or professional, real and tangible, to join a life that is less and less certain. At the inter-section of both these generosities is the same desire: to evangelize the name of Jesus Christ throughout the world. It is this zeal for evangelization which must always be the fulcrum, taken with the perspective of initial formation. The determination to dedicate one's life to evangelization for the sake of Jesus Christ and the integration of all aspects of formation in a unifying dynamic for each person, must be the criteria for the organization and evaluation of our initial formation procedures as well as any ongoing formation for formators.

(79) From this, it is worth recalling a few expectations.
- The care given to *formation communities* is essential, remembering that they must be true representatives of the life of the Order, from the apostolic perspective as well as the habitual conventual life of the Order.
- The first priority of formation is the *wholeness of the person*. Too often we realize there is a disjunction between institutional studies and other elements of this initial period. Studies become more of a scholarly career than an important part of the overall formation process of friars preachers. The subsequent difficulties which brothers have encountered in common or

apostolic life emphasize the care with which the first years must focus upon the human formation of each brother.

- If need be, provinces may benefit from examining the reasons brothers leave, in view of modifying the *criteria of discernment for vocations* (including discerning how the call to the priesthood is integrated into the religious life).
- For reasons that vary according to the particular province, we are not yet committed to ensuring that every brother of the Order, during his initial formation, has *an experience outside his province*, discovering another culture, language, ecclesial life and other method of being a friar preacher.
- Obviously, it is also essential that brothers have the chance to discover the *reality of preaching in their province*. In the same perspective, the time of initial formation must allow the chance to improve familiarity with the range of the Order's missions.
- The *promotion and accompaniment of vocations* is given various degrees of attention among the provinces. Visitations are often the chance to emphasize the importance of a pastoral ministry of vocations and the effect this has of stimulating the rest of the province. Truly we notice that vocations promotion is much better and more fruitful when it can rely on a clear definition of the principal motivations and goals of the life and mission of the province.
- *Complementary studies* should be foreseen and planned in a systematic way. This is no longer the case in certain provinces. Either we no longer see much importance in this part of the Order's mission, or most commonly we allow short-term needs to mask our preparation for the mission in the longer term.
- We should emphasize the role of the *formation councils, local and provincial*, as the place for coordination, evaluation and consolidation of the continuity between the different stages of formation. The link between the provincial formation council and the development where the province's apostolic plan should be constantly maintained so that the goal of "forming preachers" is put in the right perspective.
- The *formation of the formators* is a frequently cited need, as is the measure of the support they receive during their term and meetings with formators of other provinces.
- Too few provinces have already begun a viable process for the *formation of cooperator brothers*, at the same time adapted and integrated into the entire process of the initial formation of

every brother. In accordance with the thinking of the Chapters of Rome and Trogir, particular attention to the specific vocation of cooperator brothers is necessary perhaps more than ever today, because of the role the laity are called to play in the renewal of evangelization. Could the promotion and formation of these vocations be one of the ways in which the Order responds to the challenge of this need for renewal?

Ongoing Formation

(80) In many provinces, brothers deplore the fact that the plan for ongoing formation is so weak. The Chapter of Trogir emphasized the difficulty of devising effective initial formation in a province which did not give enough importance to ongoing formation. I acknowledge that these difficulties in respect of ongoing formation are shared by a number of Institutes. Regarding such visitations, I would like to echo what I have been told about these issues during visitations about the issues I encountered.

- Besides the importance of the conventual Lector, already mentioned above:
- Brothers often stress the need for a human formation, like that of ongoing retraining in theology envisaged by the texts of the Order, especially the Constitutions. This is never easy to implement, often due to the "availability" of the brothers, even if a great majority see the value and feel the need.
- Within the framework of the recommendation of the Chapter of Trogir, but without being able to completely respond, one of the *socii* has taken responsibility for ongoing formation in particular. In view of this, the Jubilee Year has been the chance to give the entire Order a course in *Lectio Divina*. Could this be a call to continue our "plunge into the Word?"
- Occasionally, some brothers take advantage of a "sabbatical" to benefit the teaching and research of Institutes under the jurisdiction of the Master of the Order. Could we imagine these Institutions having theological, exegetical and philosophical refresher courses for the Order's brothers in their programs?
- The desire for formation, or at least some structural accompaniment, for brothers responsible for the common goods of the community is often expressed and for links outside the Province with the entire Order (Prior, Syndic, conventual Lector...) Experiences of "best practice" could be exchanged between

provinces. In the same way, often stressed is the need to give recently ordained brothers (in their first three to five years of ministry) time for formation based upon their first experiences. We stress too the need for specific plans for cooperator brothers. It is in this context of specific proposals that the formation of formators should be placed.

- Ongoing formation would also be the chance to begin more structured collaborative programs within a region of a province, or even between provinces.

"Preaching and the renewal of evangelization"

(81) "If I proclaim the Gospel, this gives me no ground for boasting, for an obligation is laid on me, and woe betide me if I do not proclaim the Gospel!" (1 Cor 9:16). Such is the theme of this Jubilee year of celebration!

A few weeks before I wrote this report, I participated in the last Synod of bishops on the theme of the vocation and mission of the family in the Church and the world. Listening to the bishops from all over the world, made me aware of the joys and pains of their people as well as the challenges for evangelization in their dioceses. I often thought of the brothers and sisters of our Order in all these places who make their own the cry of St Paul. I recognized even more clearly the range and richness of their preaching, always rooted in a particular church and culture, but also forming one "holy preaching" in communion with all other members of the Order.

(82) Such variety is evident when we look at the conclusions of the visitations made in the last six years. There is a variety of pastoral ministries: spiritual direction, teaching and research, creativity in preaching in the digital age or through the medium of art, human and social support. There is a variety of places where such work is done: in the context of a strong Church presence or that where "secularization" is dominant, in places of peace or conflict, in well-known places or those more remote or forgotten. There is a variety of ways in which we are present: priories or houses, greatly involved in the local Church or more itinerant, contributing to church projects or not, or undertaking more specifically Dominican projects. It seems to me that this is one

of the great challenges with which we launch our Jubilee celebrations. We must find a zeal for evangelization taking so many different forms and the strength of our fraternal communion at the service of the Church in the ministry of the Word. At the heart of this variety we find the unity of the Order's preaching. How can we strengthen this and increase our own contribution to the renewal of evangelization in the Church? I think one of the major goals of the Jubilee Chapter should be to launch the preaching of the Order into the future with courage.

(83) On the basis of this rich and wonderful variety of activities of brothers preaching in all these ways, I would like in this last part of the *Relatio* to state a few points for attention which are often highlighted in meetings with brothers and in the conclusions of visitations. In so doing, as all Chapters from the beginning of the Order have done, I call for the General Chapter to reflect upon where, why and how the Order wants to send its brothers to bring their own specific contribution as preachers to the mission of the Church in the world.

"Going out to meet the other," as an apostolic response

(84) Quite often brothers mention the fact that existing communities with their current commitments (centers, parishes, institutions, historic presence, etc.) do not allow them to respond to needs they urgently recognize. This does not affect the quality and relevance of their preaching, but it does demonstrate the need for continued reflection on the part of the communities and the provinces. On the basis of an analysis of the apostolic needs and how they are met, which it is for brothers to undertake together, a community can readapt its apostolic plans. Where appropriate, they should take innovative or reorienting decisions that ask for a generosity and a trust in Divine Providence that will enable us to 'go out to the world', leaving the safety of the known for the risks and possibilities of the unknown. Such a movement of shared reflection is essential if we are to build among the brothers a sense of common apostolic responsibility, so that the ability of brothers and communities to move on (in the geographic sense, but also in terms of the priorities given to the preaching mission in a particular place) can be reviewed. Certainly, if we can come to agree together about the nature of our shared apostolic

responsibility, each brother will be able to use his own preaching talent to the better, and at the same time remain available to be called upon to change for the sake of the "common apostolic good." What are the main questions raised by the brothers and what would be likely to lead to this kind of flexibility for a renewal of our preaching mission?

(85) The first is the feeling that we must strengthen our links with those who count for little in the eyes of the world. Across the world, albeit in different ways in different countries, there are situations of great poverty and insecurity of life. The issue of respect, promotion of fundamental human rights and the integration of all in a united and cohesive society starting with the most vulnerable, is a burning issue in many places. These realities should call us to embrace in our turn the founding intuition of Dominic as he bound his own life and goals with those whose lives he considered to be in danger.

(86) A second nagging question concerns those who are distanced from the faith and/or its practice. Travelling around the Order, I feel that most of the time and energy of the brothers is dedicated to people who believe and practice. And we can be pleased about this. Nevertheless, even when our conventual or parish churches are full or our circles of friends many and energetic, this should not blind us to two realities. On the one hand, many people – in particular the youngest and among them, especially those who live far from the places we usually frequent, such as those who do not belong to a university – once they have been instructed in the faith move away and become strangers. Not only must we understand the reasons for this "estrangement," but also we must seek how to reconnect with those who now are far away. On the other hand, beyond the confines of "believing peoples," there is a much greater number who have never encountered the witness of revelation and faith. Evangelizing zeal urges us to leave those already established places to go and meet these people, in order to offer them the joyful experience of a personal encounter with Jesus Christ. This call will lead us to move on to places where the Church is most fragile, less established, not welcomed or supported, for we are very often established in "recognized" places. This is also a challenge for the Order's preaching, not only

to be of help to the Church's presence where she is quite strong and well-known, but to establish her far away.

(87) Such a concern to go out to meet people beyond the circles that are close to us calls us to take paths which will lead to fresh and different ways of starting a conversation. This attitude is also important if we want to answer the questions that are asked, both of and within the Church concerning language, which seems to keep it at a distance from that of its contemporaries. What better way is there in which to begin to understand others than to start a conversation with them? Such a call for an "exodus" from our established positions opens two perspectives in particular. The first is that of conversation with cultures with which we are not at home, like the intercultural or interreligious worlds of the deprived areas, the world of many young people, or even the world of the new social networks. The second is that of contemporary knowledge, to which, at least in the case of most of us, we are increasingly strangers. Knowledge of fields such as, contemporary philosophical currents, the modern technosciences and their influence on the relationship of the human being to themselves and their environment, herself and her environment, research into transhumanism, new digital knowledge, ecological sciences, economic and political sciences and their critics... "Let us go down on our knees and pray for understanding," as Dominic was to have said, "to enable us to understand their tongue, ...so that we may preach Jesus Christ to them" (*Lives of the Brethren,* II, 10).

(88) From this perspective of encounter, the tradition of the Order as much as the reality of the contemporary world, urges us to be especially attentive to other world religions, to the possibility of dialogue between Churches and religions as well as insistence upon the impact religious conviction and practice has upon the function of society. In many ways – whether it is current international tensions and conflicts, the radicalization of religious groups, or mutations and polarizations at the heart of the Catholic church and in relationships with other Christian churches – this directly concerns the preaching of salvation which can hardly claim to serve the conversation of God with the world without taking an active part in a "conversation of religions." Like the Church herself, and its many institutions, the Order must learn to resist the temptation to self-reference.

(89) At the beginning of his preaching, Dominic took two decisions on which to base the mission: to commit to following Christ the preacher on paths of encounter in order to preach there; and to listen to his teaching. Study and preaching are without doubt the most effective antidotes to self-reference. Once more, this emphasizes the intrinsic link our tradition aims to foster between study and preaching. A link which must be the preferred foundation both for our suggestions for initial formation of new brothers and for our programs established by the provinces for ongoing formation of all the brothers. I return here to a point that has already been mentioned. It is absolutely crucial to foster at the heart of the Order a genuine dialogue between those with a lived experience of the preaching ministry in its broadest sense, and the theologians whose reflection is rooted in the understanding of Biblical revelation and who present in fullness the doctrinal teaching of the Church. There is absolutely no doubt that to engage in this adventure would strengthen the particular ways in which the Order serves the Church.

(90) This would also be a way of acknowledging the perplexities and anxieties voiced by the brethren during visitations about the trends they notice in today's Church: a transformation in the relationship of the faithful to the facts of parish life; divisive attachments to a separate group identity within the Church community; the choice of many Catholics to join other, younger churches shaped by the Evangelical movement; the difficulty in encouraging a community dimension in the life of faith; the active place of the laity and their freedom for creative initiatives for evangelization; the role of women; a real integration of the intercultural quality of a Church increasingly effected by global-ization and population movement; difficulties the modern person meets in her relationship with an institution and her own authority... Again it has to be said that we can address these issues only to the extent to which we enter the reality and experiences of those we serve.

Questions about government for restructuring preaching in a province

(91) We know that for preaching as well as for entities and institutions of the Order, the celebration of the Jubilee invites us to commit to a

process of "restructuring" and I want now to tackle the questions about government which sometimes arise when accompanying or implementing this renewal.

(92) The issue most often raised is that of manpower. Indeed, our governing bodies in particular, when making assignations, are often faced with difficulties of "human resources" (numbers, availability, specialized skills) which do not always correspond to the need. The leadership also faces the problem of ensuring an – albeit fragile – balance of communities. However, to avoid being paralyzed by these difficulties, I feel it is useful to take the time to ask, should we speak of a lack of resources or of an ambition too great in relation to capacity? Are we talking about being willing to innovate just so long as we don't abandon anything we have already done? Or is there a failure to have a shared awareness of a plan for the mission?

(93) Another difficulty concerns the tension between the short term and long term. Thanks be to God, many of our provinces are receiving new vocations and so have the possibility of developing their apostolic activities to the full. But this renewal is happening at a time when the communities have a great number of needs to meet. In this context, we must avoid the risk of seeking to provide for these needs in the short term without giving thought to an overall long-term plan. And we must give the youngest brothers time to finish their formation and gain the experience and the qualifications that will be essential if they are to embrace in a creative and lasting way the tradition they are to hand on.

(94) As I have already noted in the preceding chapter on the life of the brothers, quite often we notice a mutual ignorance about communities, as though each community was an "island" federated with others in the same "distant" entity (a tendency we can also see in the relationship of a Province to the whole Order – or of certain brothers with their community). This has consequences for the apostolic life. Unless we confront this tendency to center upon ourselves and overcome it, it will be more and more difficult to engage in a common project within a province or a common apostolic project for the whole Order. The point to challenge, I feel, could be identified as a trend towards a kind of "federation" where the Dominican "brand" becomes more a "franchise" than an

identity, a common holy preaching that we offer all together to the life of the Church.

(95) When we speak of developing and implementing a plan for the life and mission of a Province, the question of decision-making arises: beginning a new project, giving a fresh direction to another, leaving a presence or mission, opening or closing priories and houses. Recent years have shown that this is far from easy and here I want to try to tackle what I understand of these difficulties and so make some proposals. How do we ensure that our decisions will be fruitful and meaningful for the future?

- In the case of a closure, we must acknowledge that it is never easy to leave a place where the Order has had an ancient, often "historic" presence. Many brothers have with generosity invested an important part of their lives in that place, and links have been forged with people for whom these are important reference points for their human and Christian lives. We can feel that we are abandoning something without really knowing whether something else will produce the same fruit. Quite simply, it is not easy to let go and leave, and this is even harder when we have put down roots over (too many?) years. So, it is never enough just to make a decision. It is always indispensable to stay alongside and to listen to the brothers concerned.

- Whether it is about new directions or finally leaving a place, above all, decision-making must be driven by apostolic concerns and a will to bring these concerns to the local Church where we work, aligning them with the needs identified by others. Quite often, I am surprised at the ease with which we plan either the development or the closing of our work in terms of what we think *we* should or can do, without taking the time to assess the relevance of our decisions to others or the consequences for them. Dialogue with the local church is in many cases indispensable, not only to "inform" but also to discern.

- In this way preparation for such a decision must take the time and means to inform and to listen to the people who will be affected by the change. Too often I feel the faithful are not heard, or are put in a very uncomfortable position by the brothers who themselves involve them in their tensions or disagreements. If we have a united concern for the people it allows us to examine these situations more objectively and make appropriate decisions more calmly.

- Regarding our historic places, "discernment" must take account of the varied character of these situations. It may be a place which has been and still is essential in the apostolic identity of a province; the challenge is therefore to strengthen it, even if it means leaving other less important projects. It could be a historic place for the province and/or the Order, but one where no specific activity is happening or can be made to happen. In that case we have to let ourselves be persuaded that bricks and mortar cannot be our master. Sometimes it is a place whose special historic significance is still relevant today, though we no longer have the energy or the competence to carry it on. In that case we must have the humility to hand it to others, preferring to make sure of the future work, rather than retreat into past glories as the years pass with little awareness that we are no longer equal to the task.

- Using the word "discernment" emphasizes that, when decisions must be taken in the provinces (not only for lack of forces, but also when adapting to needs) this is to be done by means of a process involving the brothers who will be affected. I notice that often we can be tempted to "take courageous decisions" because in order to be responsible we find we need to "come to a decision." There are situations where this type of decision is necessary even if it seems to some to have been taken and imposed "by force." But I feel that most often it is possible to take the time for the decision-making process, and to tackle objections and resistance calmly, even when it feels like wasting time. Once again, it is a case of encouraging the sense of common responsibility which is the foundation of our fraternal and apostolic communion. In the long term, this contributes to peace and unity.

- At the province level, it is important that decisions taken in favor of such a change of direction are free from whatever could result in changes being made in the dark – as for example, a false argument about historic value, too close a link to a brother or group of brothers, the inclination to cause a rupture (between generations, between ideologies), where none of this has any bearing on the project in question, or financial interests. Again, this is a matter of pursuing the process of discernment in an objective way. Do I need to add that to conduct such a process, our Constitutions provide plenty of guidelines to make reasoning objective and stop it from being arbitrary.

- Finally, concerning these changes of direction, I have become aware in the course of a number of visitations that quite often we think more readily in terms of our "physical presence" in a place than in terms of consolidating our potential for itinerant preaching. Very often the task of preaching is carried out in this or that place which does not require a fixed presence, for it could be carried out from another place or under different forms or sporadically, perhaps in collaboration with other places in the province. It could sometimes be more specifically linked to the mission of the Order. Taking this into consideration would in many places allow us to avoid spreading the brothers over too many small communities, where neither a life of fraternal communion nor flexibility is easily achieved.

(96) Between the shaping of a province's plan for its life and mission and the putting of this plan into action, there comes the question of collaboration between the provinces. The General Chapters of the Order, and this was already happening in the first chapters at the very beginning, should provide the occasion for the provinces to examine the key issues that concern the apostolic responsibility of the Order. In this way, brothers can create more collaborative projects between the provinces. Often we do collaborate, asking a province to come to the rescue, helping with a project that local resources can no longer complete alone. And this is good. But could we not make the idea of province collaboration a priority in our planning, not only as a "supplement" but also to strengthen the quality and specificity of the Order's universal mission within our own province? For example, if we dare believe it is not so serious to have one community or one parish fewer in a province, but important to free brothers so that the Order could undertake a particular work, or be present in a particular place (even if this is under the responsibility of another province), the mission of the entire Order could be strengthened. It is my hope that at the General Chapter of the Jubilee, we might find a way to open those paths to cross-provincial assignations so that, favoring some of today's essential missions (see above), the provinces of the Order, while safeguarding their own identity, would have the joy of participating in the universal mission of all and receiving in their turn a supplementary strength.

Questions of "identity" at the heart of the apostolic community project

(97) My meetings with communities often bring to attention the fact that since the witness to fraternal communion is an integral aspect of the preaching, we need to take practical steps to make sure of the dynamism and influence of this communion, if its life is not to be reduced to the bare minimum that is required. Listening to the brethren convinces me that we absolutely must give back to this dimension its full place in our lives, as much for the sake of the brothers' own equilibrium and joy of living and mutual support in the spiritual life, as to give us the means to live the life of preachers of the gospel. In addition to all this, our putting our faith in Christian fellowship, our determination to achieve unity by democratic means, and all we do to secure the engagement of everyone in working together for the good of all, are so many signs of which contemporary society has need.

(98) What is more, this witness of fraternity in aid of our preaching is particularly significant while we seek to establish communities in which different generations learn to live together, where cultures contribute to building a single community and different ecclesial sensibilities dialogue calmly in truth. Do I need to stress the power of the witness of simplicity and sobriety of life, where all renounce their entire private and personal economy for the benefit of holding goods in common, where all can trust that their own needs are taken into consideration? We know, it is very often this economic dimension which best reveals the authenticity of our choice of common life.

(99) Study is one of the essential observances of the Order and a central element of our identity. We are all proud of this tradition. Nevertheless, brothers often lament the little time they can dedicate personally to study outside of the minimum necessary for the needs of ministry and the great difficulty in effectively creating a culture of common study. However, our community meetings during these visitations show how it is necessary, and a tremendous help for one another, to take time to study the realities encountered daily in preaching: for example, the "defamiliarization" of the Christian Revelation and of the Church in many contemporary societies and the phenomenon of

"secularization"; the sense of multiple religious journeys or quests for wisdom which drives a number of our contemporaries; the phenomena of instrumentalization of religions in a process of identitarism [i.e. anti-globalism] or radicalization; the feeling of a growing incongruity between Church discourse and that of contemporary knowledge. Similarly, we can highlight the need for a greater familiarity with varied theological and philosophical research. Study, from this perspective, forms a solid point of departure for reading the "signs of the times" and so prepares us to adapt our preaching. What is more, that one human community takes up this challenge in the name of faith by giving a priority to study is, in itself, a sign to the world.

(100) The identity of the Order also comes from the Dominican Family in a variety of forms. This makes its demands on the brethren, who must learn to develop their collaboration with the other members of the Dominican Family to greater effect. At the heart of the Church, the reality of the Dominican Family offers the chance to bring the special contribution of a preaching borne by a "little church" made up of different states of life working together in a single family. This highlights the importance of a closer collaboration in the Dominican Family, so that everyone can bring their specific contribution to the ministry of evangelization according to his or her state of life. Still being careful to avoid any anachronism, can we say it is part of the wealth of the Order, the gift it has, to have been founded right from the beginning as a synergy between different states of life? Today, this gift is abundantly displayed, even if – as mentioned above – we must continue to think of new ways of achieving a balance within the partnership. My visits have given me an opportunity to discover very many fine examples of cooperation between friars and nuns, friars and apostolic sisters or the laity of the Order, sometimes even projects undertaken by the entire Dominican Family. But my visits also permit me to observe how it can happen that the new shoots can also grow up side by side in a climate of mutual appreciation, yet lack concerted planning when that could make them useful for the Church, for example in education, or the pastoral care of families, or in teaching and research in theology. Sometimes, they can meet real difficulties, as is sometimes the case, for example, when there are misunderstandings between the brothers and the young people of the Dominican Youth

Movement. When we talk in the Church of mobilization together for the new evangelization, (that is to say, a pastoral conversion that must change the very face of the Church in the world, in her internal relationships as much as in her way of speaking in the world) how do we get the maximum profit from the richness that exists in the Dominican Family? And again, when the need for "first evangelization" is even more noticeable, should the Dominican Family not take the time to reflect together upon the implantation of this specific service of evangelization in the word, by doing more than simply relying on the opportunities given us in certain places where brothers, sisters and laity are presently in a position to collaborate? I could give a few illustrations: a territory is particularly waiting for the Dominican charism, could we discuss how to respond to this call, at least in one branch, with occasional support from the others? Would some collaborations be possible to strengthen our work of education? How can we collaborate in the Salamanca process? Could institutions of theological teaching seek to find better ways of involving women as well as men, laity as well as religious? Projects for evangelization (in parishes or other forms) should prioritize the gospel of the family: how do we begin and develop this in dialogue with brothers and sisters, religious and laity? Clearly these questions demonstrate that the Order, following the example of the whole Church, must renew its approach to to the question of the role of families, women and lay people in the adventure of the New Evangelization.

(101) From this point of view, I think it important that we undertake a reflection in our communities and provinces upon one aspect of the identity of the Order of Preachers in view of its being a clerical Order. As such, the Order must be governed by clerics and assumes within the Church a presbyteral ministry. It is a "collaborator of the College of Bishops." Changes in the shape of the Church since the Second Vatican Council should call us to review this notion with fresh eyes. What is the significance of the presbyteral office in a collective entity? What are the ways for the Order to exercise this office, namely, to make Christ present in this world? How does this definition clarify the individual call made to brothers, under obedience, to present themselves for ordination? How can this approach lead us to think of the vocation of the "cooperator" brothers in a new way? With what and with whom are these

brothers cooperators? What are the consequences of such an approach to understanding and promoting a solidarity of preaching within the Dominican family? How do we conceive the link between preaching the Gospel and the sacramental life of the Church today (cf. LCO 1, V-VI)?

(102) In this perspective, ecclesiology and theology since Vatican II have led us to speak of the vocation of "lay brothers." Changes in the world and in the Church have led me to conceive of the lay vocation at the service of evangelization in an altogether new way. I think this calls the Order to consider anew how to integrate these changes. The Order is without doubt a clerical Order, which does not refer only to discipline. Rather, our tradition acknowledges that the dynamic of preaching the Word leads logically to sacramental celebration, beginning with that of Reconciliation. Yet, the new context of the faith in many contemporary societies along with the new status of lay people as agents of evangelization (which makes the Church what she is) makes us think how men could be called to consecrate their lives to the ministry of the Word in the Order, without having a vocation to the priesthood.

(103) To conclude this chapter on identity, I ought to mention the question of economics in relation to the planning and apostolic choices of a mendicant Order. Whether or not it is explicitly spoken of, this aspect plays an important role in the shape the apostolic life of the Order takes today. Without wanting to be too simplistic, I think that in certain cases, this aspect "blinds" our discernment and leads us to make choices about which, in the end, we are not convinced, but think will allow us to ensure economic security for the communities and for the province. Without giving a univocal opinion on this, I would like here to invite each community to assess this potential confusion in our decision-making.

Honoring the "priorities" of the Order: from preaching to theology and back

(104) Regarding the ministry of the Word, the General Chapter of Trogir took up the thoughts of the Rome Chapter by identifying key themes which could bring together mission forums, approximately covering the major ministries of brothers (Parish

ministry, education, schools of preaching, interreligious dialogue, pastoral care in the indigenous world, ministry to migrants, popular devotions and pilgrimages, new media and communication, ministry in large city centers, youth work). These mission forums would encourage apostolic activity by taking on board three areas of concern:

- Putting brothers in contact who, engaged in the same apostolic field, want to share their experience;
- Identifying what the Order's specific tradition can bring to the Church in these fields, and how we could include even more of a renewed concern for evangelization in these areas. On this, the Chapter of Trogir recalled that as well as apostolic priorities long held by the Order, we should today be particularly attentive to three areas: vulnerability, the search for meaning, and secularity.
- By means of this discernment of the real situation in which the apostolate is carried out, we might single out those themes which call for a dialogue of pastors and theologians so as to encourage a renewal of evangelization based on a theology of pastoral care.

(105) This is the dynamic exchange, by which we may examine the real situation of the apostolate today and respond to it creatively, which the Conference for the Mission wants to bring to the very heart of the Order. The preparation of this Congress, which is already underway, already assumes some of this mission. Picking up on conversations with the brethren during my visits around the provinces, I want here to raise a number of questions that concern our renewal of evangelization.

- What sort of conversation is going on between preaching and pastoral care and theology? The dialogue between theology and pastoral experience, such as that at the heart of the Salamanca process mentioned above, underlines the importance of this question for the way we put the tradition of the Order at the service of a renewed evangelization; instilling the Order's tradition in the renewal of evangelization, bringing together theology and preaching to offer the Church the service of an Order of preachers who do theology.
- How do we make teaching and research in theology of greater influence in shaping the mission of the preacher? Just as study is essential to the makeup of our communities, our tradition

considers it indispensable to the mission of proclaiming the good news of the Kingdom. So I think it indispensable to encourage a conversation between those brothers who are more specifically and fully dedicated to this task in order to improve the way we can serve the Church. Further, some brothers are charged with teaching theology or religious sciences to students from secular disciplines. This task is not easy, for dialogue with other fields is demanding. If these brothers were encouraged to reflect together this would be fruitful.

- How involved are we in the life of particular churches? Through-out all the provinces, some observations have been made: diocesan churches are structured in parishes (and we participate very well in these places), but we notice that there are more and more "parishes of choice." Even if this is not (thank God) always the case, in many places it is often lamented that young adolescents seem to disappear from the life of the Christian community once preparation for the sacraments is over, even in places where the faithful are numerous. We learn that pastors wish the faith was more consolidated, and particularly more rooted in a knowledge of the Word. Although we talk a lot about the engagement of lay people in evan-gelization, we sometimes find it difficult to get beyond the help lay people give their pastors over technical matters and share responsibility with them in any pastoral field, as well as speak-ing much of the engagement of the laity in evangelization, we sometimes have trouble to pass from "technical" support that the laity give their pastors to a real co-responsibility in certain pastoral areas. With all its experience of many cultures and its commitment to theological research, shouldn't the contribution of the Order be to offer more thoughts on all these issues?

- How do we renew our reflection on relations with the local Church? It is obvious that in most places in the world, the most "structured," "visible," and for this reason, "recognized and identified" Church, is the Church which has a diocesan structure. It is also clear quite that that, in many places, religious life is accepted in a diocese to the extent – or even on the condition – that its members (and for the brothers mostly its priests) involve themselves in the life of the local diocese (parishes, diocesan services, chaplains...). We cannot deny that our response to such demands is also motivated by the financial needs of our communities. Also, sometimes, individual brothers are "recruited," or offer their services for more "individual" reasons outside of the range of the explicit apostolic plan of the province (we can mention here brothers who say they have made this choice for lack of being asked for anything specific by their province). We should also emphasize that it would be best not to consider a house where it is the community that takes on the responsibility for a parish, in the same light as one where most of the brothers take on parish jobs quite independently of one another. Quite often during visitations, I have asked communities this question: in your opinion, what are the needs of the local Church to which the Order can make its specific contribution? And further, in view of your analysis of the situation and its needs, what proposals for apostolic initiative would you like to offer the bishop of the place? I feel that we might take more time to ask ourselves these questions, and the normal relationship with a local bishop should not be to ask him first what he proposes for this or that brother, but rather what he thinks of an initiative we want to offer the diocesan Church. Certainly, this would change our relationship with local Churches quite profoundly, what is more, this would probably transform the understanding many bishops have of religious life in the Church, first because of their ignorance, but also from the way we position ourselves in the Church. With this perspective, we return once more to consider what could be the role of a Priory of friar preachers in a diocese, with the proposal that it can be a place of "contemplative preaching," of study and the sign of fraternal communion.

- What is specific for the consecrated life? Brothers often regret that "the religious life is not acknowledged in the dioceses," but at the same time, like many other religious and consecrated, we willingly adopt a "functionalist" attitude in our diocesan involvement. What prior provincial, assigning a new brother to a community, does not go to see the bishop to ask if he has a job for him? How many times do we go to see a bishop to offer an apostolic initiative we wish to do for the particular Church?
- How are we to understand the very significant development of new Evangelical Churches in every latitude? What dialogue can we have with them? What can they teach us about renewing our zeal for evangelization?
- What qualified collective presence can we establish in this new world of social networks? It is obvious that a great number of

brothers are individually present in this world and spend time and energy there. On the other hand, collective projects are rare. These new means of communication aim to devise or promote new social networks. We sometimes wonder if, in the religious life, their use doesn't just confirm the trend for privatization of apostolic commitments. This question seems important for the Order and must be studied.

- The recent ordinary Synod of Bishops on the family confirmed that the family must be considered a major agent in evangelization. Such a statement had already been made during the Synod on the new evangelization and transmission of the faith regarding the laity and young people. How can the Order help find real ways of taking these statements seriously, through apostolic commitments and the brothers' ministries, but also through the diversity found in the Dominican Family? This returns us to the need to devise new ways for the various branches of the Dominican Family to work together on the same mission.

Some specific regional issues

This renewal of evangelization will certainly take various forms in different regions, and the reports of the socii present both the possibilities and the limits. To conclude this report, I want now to voice the issues which seem most pertinent to the different regions of the Order.

(106) *Asia and the Pacific.* This is certainly a particularly vibrant and promising region of the Order today, not only because of the many new vocations in the different provinces, but also in the great variety of human, sociopolitical and religious issues that it presents. In this region the brethren and the whole Dominican Family lay great stress on the issues surrounding the promotion of human dignity, justice and peace, in the face of the great lack of security of so many people. I feel that we should especially direct our efforts in this region to the field of dialogue between different religions and wisdom traditions. The large number of young brothers we have calls for particular attention to be paid to the process and content of initial formation. The extent and diversity which mark the majority of this region's countries must make us wary of the risk of scattering our forces, as though we put the

growth of our territorial presence above a more specific contribution of the Order. The issue of enculturation will undoubtedly be very important. Finally, China remains a great challenge for the Order's preaching, inviting us to think how we might diversify the ways in we are present in this immense country, as well as how we meet the demands of collaboration amongst ourselves.

(107) *United States.* For many years this country also has brought to the Order the blessing of many new and young vocations, allowing for a bold vision of extending the Order's charism in the future in this country and probably also through collaborations and missions abroad. The church in this country is still quite strongly marked by its missionary origin, and a challenge for the Order – which shared deeply in that era of foundations – will be to know how to anticipate the evolution of the Church in years to come. This calls on us to imagine what specific contributions the Order can bring to evangelization in this country once it gets beyond too strong an identification with "pastoral presences." Moreover, two issues seem to call especially for the development of the Order's charism today in this country. One is study and theological research in dialogue with the new knowledge which has developed there, as well as with the philosophical currents which respond to them; and the other is the particular attention to be paid to changes of religious attitudes in the country, especially those occurring with movements of migration.

(108) *Europe.* At the present time, there are three distinct regions for the Order's organization in Europe, each having its own peculiarities, particularly because of their history and the culture particular to each. However, in the perspective of a renewal of evangelization, these three sub-regions are likely to face the same challenges, if possible in interdependence on one another. The first it seems to me is the process of consolidating unity in Europe, in the different ways presently at work. Indeed, beyond a certain tendency to Euroscepticism, the brothers all emphasize the great symbolic weight of the European adventure that was born in the aftermath of the Second World War as an affirmation of the possibility of reconciliation, recognizing as it did the way religious convictions with their history are involved in the process of rebuilding Europe. The second challenge is that of the humility of

the founders. Just because the Order was born in Europe, is no longer a reason to be Eurocentric today, and the new states of equilibrium which are progressively being established call for real conversions. Thirdly, in most European countries, in which specific cultures established themselves in the course of the dialogue between Athens and Jerusalem, a trend can be seen in the "defamiliarization" of Christianity. This is happening at the same time as the emergence of a more multicultural and multireligious landscape within which Islam holds an important place. Finally, in many European countries, the Church herself is undergoing profound transformation and the question arises: how will the Order take up these challenges and make them part of its own future. Four challenges of a kind to stimulate creative evangelization?

(109) *Africa.* In Sub-Saharan Africa, the local Churches are still mostly young and growing at a great pace in countries which are themselves for the most part in a process of emerging, still marked by a very great insecurity of life, by the fragility of public and political institutions and by the persistence of historical conflicts that have often been rekindled in the aftermath of the colonial period. The Order is making solid advances in these countries and has to face the great challenge of forming the younger brothers, often with poor material resources. The challenge for the Order, given the real situation of communities, vicariates and provinces, will be to have a presence in the socio-economic and political movements of stabilization in these countries, and at the same time be engaged in consolidation and formation in the Church. A very special challenge which summons up the energies of the brothers and sisters is certainly to make the very poor their first concern, those who are an important part of the Church. From the Order's own point of view, we have to respond to two pressing needs: to promote appropriate enculturation and to ensure the real solidarity within the Order that can allow these entities to succeed in establishing themselves.

(110) *Latin America and the Caribbean* In this region the Order and the Church already have a long history, and one that is very closely linked to the way these countries are structured, their history and their cultures. In this region, too, the provinces are dynamic and radiate energy, and as in other regions they exert themselves to

ensure the primary formation of new brothers. With regard to the development of their mission, they share three principal challenges in common. The first is to be faithful to the intuitions which governed the first foundations on this continent: to have at the heart of their preaching a care for those sectors of the population that are fragile and at risk of mistreatment by interests which act against the advancement of the dignity of persons and of peoples, and which are in contradiction to the faith they show in their fine popular devotions. They have to put study and the promotion of education at the heart of their "apostolic covenant" with the people, promoting the enculturation of the gospel with respect for the indigenous cultures. The second challenge and one linked to this issue of enculturation is that of ensuring the transition from a Dominican presence marked by the era of the first missions and foundations, to the taking charge of the mission by brothers who are native to the country. The third challenge is that of the confrontation with a very intense movement of diversification within Christianity in most of these countries, and of taking up a dialogue with other churches and movements. This region is also particularly affected by the process of restructuring, with the uniting of vicariates and the change of status of certain entities (to become the provincial vicar of another province like Chile or Puerto Rico, or to prepare a vice province in the case of Venezuela, or again to put new collaborations in place between the entities of the region).

This *Relatio* is very long and I hope I have not exhausted the reader! In this Jubilee year, I have sought to reflect the efforts of all the Order's brothers to conform to the "holy preaching" in the context of the word and the Church, to ensure our common responsibility to serve the mystery and economy of the love of God for men, "evangelizing the name of Jesus Christ."

At the end of this Report, allow me to express my gratitude to many brothers who have been or are currently members of the General Council of the Curia for their precious support and their so generous contribution to the service of the Order. I would like also, asking once more your mercy, to express my profound gratitude to you, all my brothers, and to brothers and sisters of the Dominican Family, for your service to the mission of the Order, your support, your kindness and your trust.

Assuring you of my fraternal communion, I entrust to the protection of Our Lady of Preachers and to the intercession of St. Dominic the work of the next Chapter which will help us to "proclaim joyously and faithfully the Gospel of peace," and all those to whom you are bound by the ministry of preaching.

Rome, 22 December 2015

fr. Bruno Cadoré, op
Master of the Order of Preachers

Appendix II

Presentation of the General Chapter of the Order of Preachers to His Holiness Pope Francis (August 4, 2016)

Holy Father:

On behalf of the members of the General Chapter of the Order of Preachers, held in Bologna since July 16 and will conclude today with the solemn Mass of the Feast of Saint Dominic, I present to His Holiness our feeling of gratitude for giving us this audience. This meeting with His Holiness at the completion of our Chapter is particularly significant for us, even more, in this year in which we remember the confirmation by Pope Honorius III (Third) of the intuition of Dominic eight hundred years ago. In a time of profound changes for the Church and European societies, Dominic, following the guidelines laid down by the fourth Lateran Council, would propose to the Church an Order of Preachers bringing together friars, nuns and laity in the same mission that Pope Honorius III defined as "evangelization of the name of our Lord Jesus Christ." We are particularly happy to commemorate this event under the extraordinary year of Mercy His Holiness has offered to the Church, recalling that Dominic, a man of compassion and of mercy toward sinners and the poor, was often described as a preacher of grace.

The Order of Preachers celebrates a General Chapter every three years, according to three successive modalities: a chapter of diffinitors, delegates who do not have governmental tasks are elected by the provinces; followed by a chapter of priors provincial and finally a chapter which brings together priors provincial and other diffinitors and delegates elected by entities; the latter is the elective chapter.

I am pleased to present to His Holiness today the members of our Provincial Chapter, comprised of 44 priors provincial, 6 provincial vicars, the current Master of the Order and the previous Masters of the Order. This year, Father Timothy Radcliffe could not participate for reasons of health. Father Carlos Azpiroz, who is no longer a member of the chapter, asked me to convey his fraternal and respectful greeting. Also we have the custom of inviting others to join the Chapter. Among those invited are some friars of the Order: two members of the laity, cooperator brothers, in order to emphasize the importance of this specific vocation within our Order; also present is the Director of the

Jerusalem Bible School; seven members of the General Curia friars and an expert in canon law. We have also invited to this chapter some representatives of the other branches of the Order or the Dominican family, two contemplative nuns, two representatives of Dominican apostolic sisters, the International President of the Dominican Lay Fraternities, a representative of the International Dominican Youth Movement and a representative for Dominican Priestly Fraternities. We are also accompanied by a team of translators and interpreters. Given that this year we celebrate the Jubilee of the Order, I have also invited the International Commission of Nuns of the Order to hold its annual meeting in Bologna, on the same dates of the Chapter and we have also invited them to come with us today. We want to express the importance and essential place of our nuns, the part they play, from the beginning, in the mission of the Order, and which is expressed by the relationship of every nun and monastery with the Master of the Order. With all of them I express to you, Holy Father, our filial affection and our desire to serve the evangelizing mission of the Church.

In this year of the Jubilee of the Order, the preparation of the general chapter has led us to pay special attention to the call that makes us the Church and your insistence in reminding us, to renew our generosity in evangelization. Servants of the ministry of preaching evangelism, we would like to give special importance to our contribution to development of a culture of encounter, a Church of God's people on their way, encouraged by the desire to go beyond its usual circles. A Church that is a prophet of communion and unity among men, that particularly encourages participation in the life of all those who have no voice in this globalized world ruled by powers often marked by a dominant economy. The path of renewal of our vocation as preachers, members of a mendicant order, by returning to the sources of the tradition started by St. Dominic and St. Francis, has led us to emphasize three aspects: The first is the need to adjust the structures of the friars' life, communities and the provinces, so that life and mission will combine into a unified dynamic. How can the prospect of our evangelizing mission not be primarily functional (our institutions, our structures, the influence of our heritage, of our ministries ...) but have, above all, an existential dimension, which is an area of fulfillment and joy for people, an opportunity for communities to shine as "parables of communion," as Brother Roger of Taizé liked to say? Fraternal communion and hope for the world constitute the crucible of "pastoral conversion" and mutual promotion of our vocations as preachers.

The second aspect is the passion of Dominic in inscribing the ministry of the Word in a dynamic conversation, dialogue, listening and encounter. By choosing to imitate Jesus the preacher, traveling and mendicancy for the Word, Dominic wanted to contribute, to the extent possible, to the will of the Church to renew its presence in the world and its relationship with both believers and nonbelievers. His specific mode of preaching the Gospel was the brotherhood. We want those same criteria to now guide the evaluation of our evangelical and apostolic presence, as essential forms of collaboration both among the friars as well as within the family of brothers and sisters, laity and clergy of Dominic. This chapter was preceded by a pilgrimage of a hundred young students, friars, and sisters from around the world walking in the footsteps of Dominic. At the beginning of the Chapter, these young people directed a message to us, I think, that has been decisive. Their joy of belonging to an Order which is based on cultural, linguistic and social diversity, gives birth to a communion in which each stands out fully with their own gifts. In this sense, the chapter calls for developing collaboration, solidarity, international and intercultural projects.

The third aspect is made up of priorities that will guide the new initiatives that we want to undertake. Study, in that it constitutes one of the first observances of the Order, is an important criterion. A study that is situated between listening to the Word, support for profound knowledge of the tradition of the Church and concern for an open and rigorous dialogue with contemporary thought. Seeking this balance, we would like to further promote dialogue between preaching, ministries and theology, seeking to make more and more an intelligible disclosure of Truth that liberates in the midst of the conversation between God and his people. We would like to carry out this mission giving our full attention to the priorities emphasized throughout our history: encounter between cultures, dialogue with other religions, the desire to reach those who are unfamiliar with faith, friendship with the poor, abused and forgotten. How can we hear the voice of God without being challenged to hear the voice of the voiceless in this world, from whom one can truly create a human communion with the hope of salvation? Undoubtedly, one of the privileged axes of the ministry of the Word today should be to promote the participation of all, laity and clergy, women and men, consecrated or not, in the same ministry of the Word which, at the time of Saint Dominic, was called the "holy preaching."

Holy Father, the Lord gives us the grace to have at present friars in initial formation for every six friars of the Order, distributed in all regions of the world. Our biggest desire is to truly listen to what the Lord tells us in calling these young people to give their lives in service of evangelization of His Word. I express again our deep and fraternal gratitude for the confidence that His Holiness shows to us and I would humbly ask you to pray for our Order and bless us for eight centuries after its founding, that we have the courage, joy, and generosity of confirming in the world today, the intuition Dominic left us as an inheritance.

Bruno Cadoré, O.P.
Master of the Order of Preachers

Appendix III

The Pope's Address to the Dominican General Chapter

Dear Brothers and Sisters,

Today we could describe this day as "a Jesuit among friars" in the morning with you and, in the afternoon, in Assisi with the Franciscans: <a day> among friars. I welcome you and thank Friar Bruno Cadoré, Master General of the Order, for his greeting in his name and that of all those present, with the General Chapter now culminating in Bologna, where you wish to revive your roots at the sepulcher of the holy Founder.

This year has a special meaning for your Religious Family, upon the completion of eight centuries since Pope Honorius III confirmed the Order of Preachers. On the occasion of the Jubilee, which you celebrate for this reason, I join you in thanksgiving for the abundant fruits received during this time. Moreover, I wish to express my gratitude to the Order for its significant contribution to the Church and for the collaboration it has maintained with the Apostolic See, in a spirit of faithful service, from its origins to today.

And this eighth centenary leads us to remember the men and women of Faith and Letters, of contemplatives and missionaries, martyrs and apostles of charity, who took God's caress and tenderness everywhere, enriching the Church and showing new possibilities to incarnate the Gospel, through preaching, witness and charity: three pillars that guarantee the Order's future, keeping the freshness of the foundational charism.

God compelled Saint Dominic to found an "Order of Preachers," preaching being the mission that Jesus entrusted to the Apostles. It is the Word of God, which burns within and spurs you to go out to proclaim Jesus Christ to all peoples (cf. Matthew 28:19-20). The Founding Father said: "First contemplate and then teach." Evangelized by God, to evangelize. Without strong personal union with Him, the preaching might be very perfect, very reasoned, even admirable, but it will not touch the heart, which is what must change. So essential is the serious and assiduous study of theological subjects, as is all that enables

171

us to come close to the reality and put our ear in the people of God. The preacher is a contemplative of the Word and also of the people, who hopes to be understood (cf. *Evangelii Gaudium*, 154).

To transmit the Word of God more effectively requires witness: teachers faithful to the truth and courageous witnesses of the Gospel. A witness incarnates the teaching, makes it tangible, convoking, and leaves no one indifferent; he adds to the truth of the joy of the Gospel, of knowing we are loved by God and objects of His infinite mercy (cf. Ibid., 142).

Saint Dominic said to his followers: "Let us go out with bare feet to preach." It reminds us of the passage of the burning bush, when God said to Moses: "put off your shoes from your feet, for the place on which you are standing is holy ground" (Exodus 3:5). The good preacher is conscious that he moves on holy ground, because the Word he takes with him is sacred, and so are its recipients. Not only do the faithful need to receive the Word in its integrity, but also see the witness of life of one who preaches (cf. *Evangelii Gaudium*, 171). The Saints obtained abundant fruits because, with their life and mission, they spoke with the language of the heart, which knows not barriers and is comprehensible to all.

Finally, the preacher and the witness must be so in charity. Without it, they will be controversial and suspect. Saint Dominic had a dilemma at the beginning of his life, which marked his whole existence: "How can I study with dead skins, when Christ's flesh suffers?" It is the living and suffering body of Christ that cries to the preacher and does not leave him in peace. The cry of the poor and the discarded awakens, and makes one understand the compassion Jesus had for peoples (Matthew 15:32).

Looking around us, we see that today's men and women are thirsty for God. They are the living flesh of Christ, who cries "I thirst" for a genuine and liberating word, for a fraternal and tender gesture. This cry challenges us and it must be the one that supports the mission and gives life to pastoral structures and programs. Think of this when you reflect on the need to adjust the Order's organization chart, to discern the answer to be given to this cry of God. The more we go out to slake the thirst of our neighbor, the more we will be preachers of that truth proclaimed out of love and mercy, of which Saint Catherine of Siena speaks (cf. Book of Divine Doctrine, 35). In the encounter with the living flesh of Christ we are evangelized and recover the passion to be preachers and witnesses of His love; and we free ourselves of the dangerous temptation, so present today, of Gnosticism.

Dear Brothers and Sisters, with a grateful heart for the goods received from the Lord for your Order and for the Church, I encourage you to follow joyfully the charism inspired in Saint Dominic, which has been lived with different hews by many men and women Saints of the Dominican Family. Their example is a stimulus to face the future with hope, knowing that God always renews all ... and does not let us down. May Our Mother, the Virgin of the Rosary, intercede for you and protect you, so that you are courageous preachers and witnesses of the love of God. Thank you!

Francisco, Pope
Clementine Hall (Vatican Apostolic Palace)
4 August 2016

(Translation by Zenit.org)

INDEXES

General Index

www.ingramcontent.com/pod-product-compliance
Lightning Source LLC
Chambersburg PA
CBHW051041030426

42339CB00006B/138